Run To The Battle

Lessons on Spiritual Warfare

It is the Christian concept of taking a stand against preternatural evil forces. It is based on the belief in evil spirits which are able to intervene in human affairs

H.A. Lewis

Run To The Battle
Lessons on Spiritual Warfare

ISBN: 978-0-9904360-7-2   Soft cover

Copyright © 2016 by Joshua International dba
H.A.Lewis Ministries

This book was printed in the United States of
America.

Table of Contents

Chapter 1   5
  What is Spiritual Warfare?

Chapter 2   9
  Your Enemy

Chapter 3   15
  The Three Archangels

Chapter 4   19
  The Different Names of Our Enemy

Chapter 5   23
  God of Creation vs. god of this world

Chapter 6   27
  From Light Bearer to Deceiver

Chapter 7   31
  The god of This World

Chapter 8   33
  The Throne of Satan

Chapter 9   37
  How Satan Works

Chapter 10   41
  Satan's Ability to Affect The Righteous

Chapter 11
  Satan's Ability to Hinder Our Calling   51

Chapter 12   55
  Satan's Ability to Affect the Sinner

Chapter 13   67
  The Weapon of the Word of God

Chapter 14   71
  A Weapon of the Enemy

Chapter 15   75
  Jehovah God – Our Creator, Our Father

Chapter 16   79
  God is Victorious Over the Enemy's Schemes

Chapter 17   95
  The Ranks in Satan's Army

Chapter 18   103
  Everything Wrong In The World – An Act of God?

Chapter 19   109
  Resist the Devil and He Will Flee From You

Chapter 20   121
  Obey the Lord and Stand Firm

Chapter 21   131
  Whose Report Will You Believe?

CHAPTER 1

.....What is Spiritual Warfare?.....

For we wrestle not against flesh and blood, but against principalities, against powers, against the rulers of darkness of this world, against spiritual wickedness in high places.
Ephesians 6:12

And there was war in heaven: Michael and his angels fought against the dragon; and the dragon fought and his angels, And prevailed not; neither was their place found any more in heaven. And the great dragon was cast out, that old serpent, called the Devil, and Satan, which deceiveth the whole world: he was cast out into the earth, and his angels were cast out with him.

(Revelation 12:7-9)
(Cf. Genesis 3:1, 2;
(Peter 2:4; Jude 6)

What is spiritual warfare? Spiritual warfare is exactly what it says. It is a battle in the spiritual realm between good and evil. It is a spiritual war that involves everybody. The enemy cannot defeat you if you have joy. It is our relationship with God that gives us this joy. However, when you begin to do things for God, as a chore you begin to lose your relationship and defeat is imminent.

According to ***Revelation 12:7-9***, there is an actual war that is to come. In this war Michael, the great prince of Israel, raises up against the great dragon called the Devil or Satan. Michael casts him out of heaven. When he is thrown out of heaven this time, this great dragon will be bound to the earth. He will no longer be allowed access to the heavens, not even to the second heaven where his throne is now.

He will no longer be allowed to come before the Lord to accuse the brothers and sisters of their failures or sins. We fortunately have an advocate who defends us to the Father. His name is Jesus, our great High Priest who makes intercession for us forever.

The first part of the war takes place in the heavens. The next part takes place on the earth. The battle here on earth takes place on three battlefields, which is your mind, your body, and your spirit.

The enemy can really wreck havoc in your the mind. In fact the mind is one of the greatest battlefields. Though he can plague the body, he can convince you through your mind that you are not where you should be spiritually or where the Word of God says you should be. He can take you prisoner once more through your emotions into spiritual prison and torment.

He can take you away from the victories the Lord has provided for you. Most of the battle is fought in your mind. If you don't really believe this, then consider how many times you have found yourself arguing with your mind?

How many times have you wanted to do something?

....

Maybe you wanted to pray or to study God's Word, but some thoughts keep entering your mind. You begin to debate with yourself. What actually is taking place? Are you arguing with yourself or are you fighting against an unseen enemy? Nine times out of ten you are really battling with an unseen enemy. Who is trying to keep you from doing that which will help you to mature in the Lord?

Another battlefield is in your body. Now your body is from the earth. It is clay and it is very earthly minded. It will never be redeemed, and it will never get to heaven in its present condition. The enemy, because he is still the prince of this world and the god of this world, comes against the unredeemed.

The deed to this world was actually given over to Satan when Adam sinned and disobeyed God. Also because of our own foolishness and disobedience to the word of God, he can come against us, and we essentially give him the right to plague our body. We need to line our bodies up with the word of God. The Bible tells us to line our bodies up with our mind, and our mind with our spirit, and our spirit to the Holy Spirit. This is the final battleground. The devil pits his unclean spirit against your spirit; however, if you are wise, you'll place your spirit under the Holy Spirit and the battle ceases there.

- FACE THE GATES AND GAIN VICTORY

CHAPTER 2

.....Your Enemy.....

First of all we must come to understand that our enemy is not the person sitting next to us in the pew.

It is not your brother, nor your sister, neither is it the person who you work with or go to school with. Neither is it the person who stole your parking spot at the outlet store. It is not even those who say they do not believe in Jesus. You must understand that no man on the face of the earth, no matter how much they disagree with you, is your enemy.

You have one enemy whose goal is to enslave you, to destroy you, and to bring you into captivity. His name is Lucifer. He is out to do whatever he can to steal from God. He is out to take God's kingdom, God's authority and His property. If you are born again then you belong to God. You are His property. If you have been redeemed and are Spirit-filled, the enemy wants to take you from God.

Satan will do everything he can to bring the battle to you. He will lie to you. He will try to deceive you. He will attempt to ensnare or entrap you. He will plague you day and night. If you don't know the word and it isn't in you or if you don't have on the armor of the Lord, then you cannot stand against the onslaught of the enemy.

Unlike a physical enemy, you cannot see this one. He is invisible. You don't know which direction he is coming from; however, you can feel it. You feel the results of it and you can see the effects of it. It's sort of like wind. You can't see it, though you can feel it. And you really don't understand where the wind is coming from until you see the proof of it. It is the same way with Satan.

You don't know you are under attack or from which direction it is coming from until you feel the assault on your person. Now, is Satan real or is he some kind of myth that people have made up? Is he something the church uses to scare people?

The Bible speaks clearly of who Satan is. In fact *Isaiah 14:11-16* gives you kind of an idea of what Lucifer was like before he fell.

Thy pomp is brought down to the grave, and the noise of thy viols: the worm is spread under thee, and the worms cover thee.
How art thou fallen from heaven, O Lucifer, son of the morning!
How art thou cut down to the ground, which didst weaken the nations! For thou hast said in thine heart, I will ascend into heaven,
I will exalt my throne above the stars of God: I will sit also upon the mount of the congregation, in the side of the north: I will ascend above the heights of the clouds;
*I will be like the most High. (Cf. **2 Thessalonians 2:4**)*
Yet thou shalt be brought down to hell,
*to the sides of the pit (Cf. **Matt 11:23; Acts 12:23**)*

*They that see thee shall narrowly look upon thee, and
consider thee, saying, Is this the man that made the earth to
tremble, that did shake the kingdoms;*
Isaiah 14:11-16

Ezekiel also speaks of Lucifer and his position
before his fall from grace.

*Moreover the word of the Lord came unto me, saying, Son
of man, take up a lamentation upon the king of Tyrus, and
say unto him, Thus saith the Lord God; Thou sealest up the
sum, full of wisdom, and perfect in beauty.*
*(Cf. **Ezekiel 27:3**)*
*Thou hast been in Eden the garden of God; every precious
stone was thy covering, the sardius, topaz, and the
diamond, the beryl, the onyx, and the jasper, the sapphire,
the emerald, and the carbuncle, and gold; the workmanship
of thy tabrets and of thy pipes was prepared in thee in the
day that thou wast created.*
*Thou are the anointed cherub that covereth; and I have set
thee so: thou wast upon the holy mountain of God; thou
hast walked up and down in the midst of the stones of fire.*
*Thou wast perfect in thy ways from the day that
thou wast created, till iniquity was found in thee.*
Ezekiel 28:11-15

Let's take a moment and get a vision of what God is
saying here about Lucifer. You have never seen anything
here on earth in the physical as beautiful as Lucifer was
when he was created.

In fact, Lucifer's name means the container of the
glory of the Lord, the light bearer or the shining one. It was

a name given to him before he fell. The name was given to him to show his beauty and glory, which was given to him by God. The Lord said that the sum of or the fullness of wisdom was within him.

Before he fell the only being greater than him in beauty, wisdom, and power was the triune God: Father, Son, and the Holy Spirit. However, Lucifer was the greatest of all God's creation before pride reared its ugly head. And he gave it all up because of his arrogance.

What can pride do to a person's life? It can rob you of everything you have in your life, every good and wonderful thing you have. Every gift God has given you will be lost if you let pride get its roots in you. The gift will either be perverted or destroyed. You will end up like Lucifer did.

Therefore thus saith the Lord God;
because thou has set thine heart as the heart of God;
behold therefore I will bring strangers upon thee, the
terrible of the nations: and they shall draw their swords
against the beauty of thy wisdom, and they shall defile thy
brightness.
Ezekiel 28:6, 7

God has a way of dealing with rebellion. He will not tolerate it. God simply will not put up with it. In Ezekiel we see how God deals with Lucifer when He says that by the multitude of thy merchandise they have filled the midst of thee with violence, and thou hast sinned; therefore I will cast thee as profane out of the mountain of

God: and I will destroy thee, O covering cherub, from the midst of the stones of fire. (*Ezekiel 28:16*)

God is not going to permit the foolishness of Lucifer. I have no sympathy for him; although, rock groups like Black Sabbath and The Rolling Stones have tried to get us to feel that way with a song called Sympathy for the Devil. I know the devil quite well and I know what his plan is. His plan is to destroy everything that is good, pure, and righteous and to bring man into captivity.

It is truly amazing when we look at who Lucifer really is and yet the Bible states that the sum of wisdom, the fullness of wisdom was in him before he fell. In some ways it can also be confusing. How could someone so full of wisdom be so foolish? It is like Solomon, the wisest man whoever lived. He was wise but he fell by the temptations of his pagan wives. Thus, Solomon became the wisest fool there ever was on the face of the earth. In a way he was a shadow or a type of Lucifer.

Satan had all this wisdom, all this knowledge, and all this glory. Every thing that anyone would ever want, Lucifer had within him. By him giving it all up, he proves to be the wisest fool of all times.

He gambled on an impossible odd. There was no way he could have, as a created being, overthrown his creator. We don't know how long Lucifer was in front of the throne of God guarding it and leading the angels in worshipping, praising, and giving glory to God. We understand he was there. And it may have been for thousands upon thousands upon thousands of years.

He was there in the very beginning when God the Father, and the Son, and the Holy Spirit spoke all of creation into existence. God spoke the word and creation came out of nothingness. He took a planet that was completely without form and void, reformed it, and made of it the marvel we call the earth. And he did it within six days of creation.

God spoke and chaos was brought into order. He spoke and the waters were separated from the earth and the heavens. Stars came into being and the sun came into existence. The great waters of the earth found boundaries they could not cross because God spoke, "This far and no farther."

He spoke and mountains appeared and the grass and trees sprung up from the ground. He simply spoke and every kind of animal imaginable suddenly existed. When He created man He formed and fashioned him from the dust of the earth. Then the most amazing and wonderful thing happened, God breathed His very own spirit into man giving him life and man became a living soul.

Lucifer saw it all. He saw the power of God's word, never mind the power of His right hand. According to scripture the power of God's great right hand is the indication of the full majesty, power, and might of the Godhead. Instead Lucifer heard God speak and He brought order out of chaos and creation out of barrenness.

CHAPTER 3

.....The Three Archangels.....

Before man was created, God created all of the angels, including Lucifer. It was by God's spoken word the sons of God (angels) came into being. How could Lucifer have ever considered that he could have won a battle against his own creator? What drove him? What possessed him to think he was more powerful?

When we do something crazy, or something stupid and foolish, we say the devil made me do it. We blame a lot of things on Satan, but who does Satan have to blame for his foolishness just himself? He lost everything. He lost that special relationship and wonderful fellowship with God. He lost the honor of standing before the throne of God and the ability to lead all of heaven in praise and worship. He became an outcast.

When you war against God you will never win. When you determine in your heart that you are going to resist God, your battle against God is just as foolish as the devil's battle against God was. Despite whether you are a believer or a nonbeliever, if you feel Lucifer was foolish for taking the chance to war against the Lord by resisting him and trying to overthrow the Lord and his kingdom; then you have to agree with me that with you constantly resisting God and His plans for your life and well being, you are just as foolish as Satan is and you are going to end up paying the same price as the devil paid, which is eternal separation from God.

Scripture says Lucifer was one of the cherubim, or an archangel. I prefer to use the word archangel. God created three angels (archangels) greater than all the other angels in power, might, and office (authority). These three archangels were Lucifer or actually his name at this time was Heylel (*Strong 1966*) in the Hebrew, Michael, and Gabriel.

The archangel, Michael, is a warrior of God. His name, *Micha* means 'warrior' and *El*, the name God first revealed to man, means 'God'. When we combine *Micha* and *El* together we have the true meaning of the name which literally translates 'warrior of God', Michael.

The archangel, Gabriel, is a messenger of God. *(Daniel 8:16, Luke 1:6)* *Gabri* means 'messenger' and *El* means 'God'. When we combine *Gabri* and *El* together we have the true meaning of the name which literally translates 'messenger of God', Gabriel.

The archangel who fell was Heylel. In the Greek his name is translated as Lucifer, the son of the morning. *Heyl* means 'the container of the glory or light' and *El* means 'God'. When we combine *Heyl* and *El* together we have the true meaning of the name in Hebrew which literally translates 'the container of the (Shekinah) glory or light of God'. In other words it also means the reflection of the image of God.

The very glory of the Godhead was on Lucifer.

He was like a mirror that reflected back to the throne of God His glory. What an awesome position to have! He was higher in authority than either Michael or Gabriel, and he gave it all up. I keep returning to this thought because it amazes me what sin does to the nature of a created being.

Pride and rebellion caused Heylel to no longer be what he his name said he was. Michael and his warring angels fought with Heylel and his worshipping angels and they were cast out of heaven.

No longer would he be the container of the glory or light of God. Instead his name changed to Satan who was now the adversary, the enemy, or the devil.

No longer would he be the container of the glory or light of God.

Instead his name changed to Satan who was now the adversary, the enemy, or the devil

Heylel means the container of the glory of God.

The believers in Christ as worshippers take his place!

CHAPTER 4

.....The Different Names of Our Enemy.....

Revelation 12:7-8 refers to Satan as a dragon. Isn't it interesting how dragons are in every culture of the world? They are especially important in Oriental culture from places like China, Japan, Korea, and the Philippines. To them the dragon is an awe-inspiring beast. His power and wisdom is unlimited. The story or the myth of the dragon is that all other forms of creation fear the dragon.

Scripture refers to Satan as a dragon because of the intensity of its power and the nature Satan has. Therefore the dragon portrays him better than any form of creation can ever portray him. Outside of Jesus, the blood of the Lamb, the name of Jesus, and the Word of God, there is no weapon that can stop the forces of Satan.

If it weren't for the leash God has put on Satan, he would have destroyed this world a long time ago. Thank God Satan is on a short leash and can do only what he is allowed to do. We need to comprehend and recognize him as a foe. If you do not know your enemy, he will consume you.

In *Revelation 12:7-8* Satan is a dragon but *Luke 4:6* and *John 14:30* refer to him as the prince of this world. This indicates that he is in a position of authority and leadership. He is someone in control. Remember that the only position greater than a prince is a king. Though a prince rules, it is only by his father's authority. And because of his father's authority, name, and position, a prince cannot be challenged by anyone but the king.

Satan may be the prince of this world but there is one greater than he. It is the King of kings. The devil rules and reigns but he rules and reigns with limitation upon him because He who is greater than him has put these limitations on him. For a season he is free, but there is a day coming very shortly where he will be confined to the pits for a thousand years.

At the end of a thousand years he will be loosed for a season. Only God knows the length of time this season is, but at the end of this time Satan along with everyone else who rebelled against God as well as hell will be cast into the lake of fire where they will be tormented forever.

In *2 Corinthians 4:4* he is proclaimed as the god of this world. Now this is an interesting title. When we are **not** referring to *El Shaddai* or *Jehovah Nissi* or any other name of *God*, the word god means judge. Scripture says, 'are ye not all gods'. According to the Hebrew translation it literally means 'are you not all judges'. And no, you do not judge. The word used here refers to God, not the judge of the world, or even to the ruler of this world.

No matter how we define the titles given to Satan, because of Adam's fall, he has legal right to the title – god of this world. When Adam sinned Satan instantly had a legal access to do what he wanted to do to this world. Adam took what was given to him by the Lord, and gave it over to the adversary. He forfeited all of his rights and ownership to Satan, making Satan legally – the ruler of this world. As the god of this world, Satan will be in charge of everything, until the day Jesus sets up His kingdom here on the earth and once and for all take his power away from him.

Now on Calvary Jesus defeated Satan. He took the keys of death, hell and the grave from him. When He was resurrected.

He also took all of Satan's power and authority. Do not be deceived! Satan still reigns; however, he has limitations and he is under God's thumb. He is still the god of this world until all scripture and its prophecies are fulfilled.

He also took all of Satan's power and authority. Do not be deceived! Satan still reigns; however, he has limitations and he is under God's thumb. He is still the god of this world until all scripture and its prophecies are fulfilled.

CHAPTER 5

.....God of Creation vs. god of this world.....

Isn't it interesting that whenever something happens on this planet, like hurricanes, tornadoes, floods, and a massacre of innocent lives we blame God for it? In fact the insurance companies will label such things as 'an act of God'. They try to blame it on the God of creation. Oh yes, it is an act of god, but not the God of creation. It is the destructive acts of the ruler of this present world.

The insurance companies, like some religious denominations, try to portray God the Father as an angry God, who every once in a while gets fed up with mankind and causes a disaster to happen. If this were true and God got that angry, there would be nothing left of the earth. It isn't God. It is the adversary out to destroy all that he can.

We need to completely understand that the God of the Bible loved us so much He sent His Son to die for us. He is not a crude vengeful Deity. He is a God of mercy and compassion, and He will only send judgment when mercy and grace fails to get our attention. It is the rebellious nature of man which brings judgment down on us.

When we study the names or titles given to the enemy, we begin to understand his attributes and the overall makeup of his nature. Then we will realize where all these terrible events are coming from, and we will quit blaming the God of creation for these terrible acts. Instead we need to run to the God of creation because He is absolutely the only one who can protect us from these deeds.

As I have stated before Lucifer is still the god of this world with limited power. Therefore, if we truly believe in the Lord and His word, are under the blood of the Lord Jesus, are redeemed and bear His name, and are truly children of God, then God protects us and we can resist the devil. More importantly he has no power over us. If we do not know God, we have no protection. We need to come to God and surrender to Him and give our lives to the Lord.

When we see all these terrible things occurring: wars and rumors of wars, death, famine, starvation, sickness like the increase of aids, addictions, alcohol, child abuse, wife abuse, rape, murder, and robbery, how can we contribute it to the God of creation?
All the insanity going on in the world today belongs to the god of this world. He cannot help but produce this kind of evil destructive acts or effects because it is his very nature to do so.

He is filled with anger, bitterness, hatred, and jealousy. He is so vile that whatever he touches becomes contaminated, impure, dirty, and offensive. It is chaotic and disastrous. The devil is a spiritual leper and whatever he touches deteriorates and wherever he goes he spreads his spiritual uncleanness.

Whenever he sees something that is holy, that is righteous, that is pure, that is edifying, and that is uplifting, he finds a way to destroy it. If it brings unity, joy, peace, or happiness, it makes him angry and since this is his world he will do whatever he can to remove any evidence of the God of creation from it.

The adversary is real and has been around for a long time, and he will be around for a little while longer. He will do everything he can to trick us and to deceive us so he can destroy us. He wants to torment us and to make us suffer as much as he can in this life and to have us cast into hell in the life that is to come. He desires to bring sadness into our lives by destroying our loved ones and everything we love. He yearns to enslave our loved ones and us by putting heavy burdens on us and making us outcasts forever.

Before reading any further I ask that you examine your life. Do you find yourself ensnared in the enemy's trap? You can turn your life over to the Lord right now. Ask Him to cover you with His blood and to be your strong tower, your shield, your covering, and your protector. There is nothing which can stop the force of the enemy except God.

I am not trying to build the enemy up to make him more than what he is. I am trying to show that without Christ in our lives we have no chance against this enemy. We cannot see him when he strikes. He is invisible, we don't know where or when the attack will come, and we cannot prepare ourselves for his assault or his attack. (*Ephesians 6:10-18*)

There is no way we can ready ourselves and even if we could we would not have the strength to stand against him. We could not train ourselves to stand against him. We need the strength of God the Holy Spirit and the power of God's Word. We need the protection of God's only Son not only to stand against him, but to also defeat him once and for all in our lives.

CHAPTER 6

.....From Light Bearer to Deceiver.....

Satan is an extremely powerful enemy. Did he just appear one day out of nowhere? Where did he come from? What was his original position?

As previously mentioned before *Ezekiel 28:11-14* shares all the beauty and blessings Lucifer had before he fell. He was truly an awesome creation. He directed all the other angels in worship and praise. In essence, he was the worship leader of heaven with musical instruments sown in him. Precious stones like diamonds, rubies, emeralds, carbuncles or garnets and pearls were his covering. Silver, gold, and everything we consider of great value and beauty was in him.

He alone stood before the throne of God like a bodyguard. Don't misunderstand; God does not need a bodyguard. To better comprehend what it means, we have to look at the protocols within a royal court.

In England there is a person who stands before the throne of the monarchy. Of course he stands before the throne both literally and figuratively. Absolutely no one can see the king or queen unless they first have an audience with this person. There are no exceptions so it doesn't matter whom you are or what title you may hold. To visit the king or queen, an audience with this person must happen first.

When you meet with this person who stands or rather guards the throne, you state your name, your position, and the reason why you want to visit the king or queen. Once you've answered all of his questions to his satisfaction, he goes to the king or queen and tells him or her everything you have just explained to him. If the king or queen does not want to meet with anyone then you will not have an audience with the monarch; however, if he or she gives their permission then you have an audience with them. The person who stands before the throne will then escort you into the throne room before the king or queen. Once you have finished your business he will escort you back out.

This was Lucifer's position before his fall. For instance, when Michael or Gabriel came in to the throne room, Lucifer would announce them to the Lord. He would ask the Lord, "Would you like to see them?" The Lord would answer, "Yes or not right now". Nobody got past Lucifer to the throne of God, unless God gave permission.

The position Lucifer had was a very wonderful position to have. He had a lot of favor. Even his name, Lucifer, was especially favorable. In the Hebrew language names are very important because they are given to show personality strengths and sometimes weakness in a person. Names reflect the good or the not so good. I

Heylel (Hebrew) or Lucifer (Greek) was the name given to him after he was created. It meant the reflection of the container of the glory of God. In other words he was like a celestial mirror. All the majesty, the power, the strength, and the holiness, which are the very attributes of the Godhead, were reflected in Lucifer before he fell.

No wonder he was so beautiful, so glorious and so far above his brethren. He was continually being bathed in the glory of the triune Godhead. What an awesome being he must have been. The other angels must have looked on in amazement at him.

When he fell it had to have shaken heaven. All of his power, all of his prestige and honor was sacrificed for nothing, for a battle he could never have won, for a victory that he would never have. His name changed from Heylel or Lucifer to Satan. He went from being the light bearer to becoming the deceiver. He went from being the glorious of all creation to what he is now, a symbol of evil, and the ultimate symbol of sin.

There is utterly no comparison between who he was before the throne of God to who he is now. He is a broken shell and a hollow husk filled with darkness and reflecting nothing. Ironically, he believes he is still the same. He believes his own lie. He believes that someday he will conquer God.

Personally, I believe the devil has to have brain damage. He really does. To honestly and truly believe, even now after all the times he has been defeated, that he is going to win. He still believes he is going to overthrow the Godhead and establish his throne above God's. It is incredible! I don't know what he needs to have happen for him in his life to prove to him that he is going nowhere but down. Unfortunately for him it's a hopeless case.

Regrettably, there are some of us who have the same nature in us. God is constantly trying to reach out to us and speak to us in love. He is trying to show us that we are drifting away from Him and that there is no future outside of His will and calling. Instead, we still shake our little tiny fist in the face of a merciful, loving God and we tell Him we don't need Him.

We think we can do it on our own and in our own strength. We make ourselves a god unto ourselves. In reality we are guilty of the same sin Lucifer was guilty of. He shook his fist in the face of God and said, "I don't need you. I will be greater than you. I will exalt myself and place my throne above yours."

His foolishness didn't help him to gain anything. Instead he was cast out of heaven and lost every wonderful gift that was his. Be careful! Eventually he will end up in the lake of fire because of that attitude, and if you don't change your attitude as well, you will end up there with him.

CHAPTER 7

The god of This World

I made reference to Lucifer in *2 Corinthians 4:4* as the god of this world. This title provokes a question – where did he get the right to be called the god of this world? To answer this question we must look again at Creation.

In Genesis we read how God created the earth. He brought the earth out of nothingness and gave it light. He placed the sun, and the stars in the sky. He caused the fish to come to the waters, the birds to fly in the air, and the animals to walk on land. Then we read of His greatest creation. It is definitely the one He was most proud. He shaped it with His own hands from the dust of the earth and made it in his own image. He gave this being He created the name Adam and breathed into him His own breath and His own spirit. Then God placed Adam in the special garden He had created for him.

To this created earthly being named Adam, God gave him authority over all that He had just created. And the privilege of naming the things created by God was also given to Adam. Although man had authority over every creature on the earth, the only limit God put on him was that he could not eat from the tree in the midst of the garden. This tree was the tree of knowledge of good and evil.

God told Adam, "Do not take of this tree for in the day that you do you shall surely die." Adam had the right to eat of any of the other trees in the garden just not this one.

Essentially Adam was given the ruler ship of this world by God. This means Adam had absolute authority of everything in and on this world. In other words Adam was given the key to the kingdom of this world.

Then Adam listened to Eve who listened to the serpent and they ate from the one tree they were told not to. By their disobedience, they turned all of this authority over to Satan. The key was handed over and our adversary became the god of his world. His ruler ship was legal because man gave it to him. Mankind immediately became the slaves of this new dictator of the earth.

How tragic! The greatest of God's creation that were meant to be sons and daughters of God were now the slaves to a created being. He ruled legally. Because of man's terrible choice, Satan became known as the god of this world.

CHAPTER 8

The Throne of Satan

If you are a king then you have a throne. Where is Satan's throne? Not only is he known as the prince or god of this world, but he is also known as the prince and power of the air.

When Lucifer was cast out of heaven, he was cast down to the atmosphere around the earth known as the second heaven. This is where the planets, stars, galaxies, and all of the vastness of space are. Contrary to popular belief the devil's throne is not in hell. He has never been in hell, and he will never end up in hell. The scriptures state that hell and all that there is within it along with the devil, false prophet and the antichrist as well as everyone who refuses to believe in Jesus shall be thrown into the lake of fire where they will be forever and ever.

The devil's final destiny is not hell it is the lake of fire. If his throne is not in hell then he does not rule from hell. In John Milton's epic poem, *Paradise Lost*, the adversary is as a wonderful rebel ruling from his throne in hell. This is completely false. The only spirits in hell are the angels that left their first estate and are so wicked and evil that they have been chained in the lowest level and are not allowed to wander until the time of the tribulation when they are loosed for a season.

I want to reiterate this fact – the devil is NOT in hell. Hell is the prison house for rebellious souls. When man dies in his sins, he cannot go into the presence of God because of his sin. Sin separates you from God and once man is judged, he is sent straight to hell to await his final judgment. Hell may be a prison house but it is also a place of great torment with no hope of deliverance.

As terrible as hell is, it is not the final place of judgment. The final place of judgment is the lake of fire. This is the place where every sinner will be cast into along with the devil, the antichrist, and the false prophet. They will spend the rest of eternity separated from God and in horrific torment. What a reward for the wicked! We do not want any part of this.

If Satan's throne is not in hell, then where is it? It is in the heavens where he rules with the principalities and the powers and the wicked spirits in high places. Oh yes, Satan does have an army under him. This vast army consists of one-third of the angels in heaven who was cast out with him. These fallen angels are his lieutenants, captains, majors, and sergeants. They are his rulers that rule with him.

They are what you refer to as the strongmen. They rule whole nations, cities, towns, villages, and churches, even your families. It is their assignment to being chaos, destruction and confusion, and to resist and hinder the growth of the kingdom of God on the face of the earth. They will use whatever means necessary to accomplish this goal.

Besides Satan and the fallen angels you have the unclean spirits, the spirits of infirmity, spirit of blindness, deaf and dumb spirits, spirits that causes lameness, and epilepsy. These ruling spirits work under the leadership of these strongmen to torment, trouble, and to enslave mankind.

Lucifer's throne will some day be cast down to the earth from the heavens. This will happen in the future at the time of the Great Tribulation, during the last seven years before the Millennium. When Satan is cast down to the earth, the book of *Revelation* gives a warning to the inhabitants of the world.

Woe to you for the great dragon has been cast down to you and he is angry and resentful and will do everything he can to destroy and enslave the human race. *Revelation 12:9*

We do not want to be here when this takes place.

We don't want to be on the earth when the throne of Satan is moved from the second heaven to the earth itself

CHAPTER 9

.....How Satan Works.....

Satan works in the lives of believers as well as unbelievers. He divides families by turning the husband against the wife, daughters against the mother, sons against the father, mother in-laws against the son or daughter in-law and on and on. How does he work? What are his intentions?

Just as God's attributes make clear his nature, power, majesty and glory, so Satan's attributes show his character and plans for mankind. Those of us who are born again, Spirit-filled, and covered with the blood should be manifesting the nature of our heavenly Father. People shouldn't even have to ask if we are born again. The fruit of the Holy Spirit should be so evident that when people meet us they know whom we belong to.

The fruit of the Spirit, which should be manifested through us, are love, joy, peace, gentleness, longsuffering, goodness, faithfulness, meekness, and temperance. We should be someone who people just want to be around. There should be something about us that people just want to reach out and touch us. They want to be like us. They want to follow us as we follow Christ.

Because we are children of God, we should have so much of God's nature in us that people will have a hard time seeing the difference between Jesus and us. Naturally we cannot become Jesus, but we can get to be a lot like Him. When the fruit of the Spirit is manifested in our lives, people will see the essence of Jesus.

Whenever we arrive anywhere, people will be glad because when we come we bring heaven with us. Wherever we put our feet, we cause it to become God's property. Just as the Lord told Joshua, "every place that the sole of your foot shall tread upon, that have I given unto you." *(Joshua 1:3)*

God does this because He knows that we will establish God's kingdom on the earth, not ours. We establish God's way and God's will everywhere we go. It is just the new nature of the born again believer to be this way.

Just as we have God's nature, the children of the god of this world also manifests his nature like his anger, his resentment, his bitterness, his foolishness, his jealousy, his rage, his hate, and his prejudices. Wherever he goes he does not edify, lift up or build up. He tears down, destroys and divides. Chaos and fear follows every place he goes.

Sickness, trouble, and pain follow him. Agony, hurt, loneliness, despair, and hopelessness abound. No matter where he goes anything that can bring man into bondage and shame is there. It is his very nature. And his destructive nature will be manifested through his children.

He steals because he is a thief. He lies because he is the father of lies. He kills because he has been a murderer from the beginning. He commits adultery and he rapes because it is his nature. He is a fornicator – it's just who he is. Just like the spots on a leopard tell us it is a leopard, Satan's nature tells us that he is a devil and his children are just like him.

Wherever his children go they establish his kingdom and bring the same chaos, the same spiritual storm, the same destruction, the same bitterness, and the same seeds of discord. Just as we know the devil by his works, we know the devil's children by their fruits. No matter how hard we try we cannot hide the fruit in our life.

We can proclaim to be an apple tree all day every day but if oranges are growing on our limbs, an apple tree we are not. Just because we say it doesn't make it true. We only know the truth because of the kind of fruit that is shown. The fruits we have manifested in our lives portray our nature. They are the evidence that show who we really are.

If we interact with others everyday with anger, bitterness, hate and jealousy, or curse and swear, then we cannot proclaim to have the fruits of the Spirit in us. This kind of fruit shows we belong to the god of this world, not the God of creation. However, if there is chaos and destruction around us, but we bring peace, restoration, and healing, then the fruits of our heavenly Father is showing through us and the evidence of the Holy Spirit is being manifested in us and no matter what man may say about us the fruits will show we are children of God.

pg. 39

In *John* the Lord said that all men would know the disciples were His because they have love for one another. It is through the fruits of the Spirit all men will know we are the disciples of God.

CHAPTER 10

.....Satan's Ability to Affect The Righteous.....

In *Job 1 and 2* we have the opportunity of observing a meeting between the sons of God and Satan. And we see God speaking of His love and appreciation for Job. He makes a very wonderful statement about him. He informs Satan that there is no one like Job on the earth. He says Job is blameless, upright, fears God and turns away from evil.

Now God tells Satan this after He asks, "have you considered my servant Job?" Satan replies that Job is like this only because God shelters and protects him. God has him hedged in. In the today's language Satan said to God, "Allow me to put my hands on him. Let me test him. You will see how fast he curses you to your face."

There have been many sermons preached on why the Lord allowed this to happen to a righteous man. The Lord, Himself bore witness to Job's faithfulness. Why? Why allow this to happen? This is where we must have faith in God and in His wisdom. We must trust that He knows what He is doing.

Of course we know the outcome of Job's testing, he received double of what he lost. Understanding our human nature, I can guarantee Job would have preferred not to be tested at all. As soon as we feel we are being put to the test, many of us today begin to beg God to deliver us.

We forget the words of Peter in *1 Peter 4:12, 13* when he says, "Beloved, think it not strange concerning the fiery trial which is to try you, as though some strange thing happened to you. But rejoice, in as much as ye are partakers of Christ's suffering, that when His glory is revealed, ye may be glad also with exceeding joy."

Rejoicing in hardship is definitely against our human nature. We do not want to suffer, especially if we feel we are innocent. As soon as we feel we are being tested or attacked by Satan, we cry out to God for deliverance. We become consumed with fear and anxiety and plead with God to deliver us from the test. What we should do is ask Him to help us be developed into what God wants us to be, not to be delivered from what He has allowed in our lives.

If God delivers us from what He sent our way to strengthen and not to destroy us, then He will have to test you again later on down the road. The problem is that we will be weaker and the test will be stronger. However, if we let God develop us in the image of His Son, then we will be stronger and the enemy will not choose to challenge us in that way again.

1 Peter 3:12 says that the eyes of the Lord are over the righteous, and his ears are open unto their prayers: but the face of the Lord is against them who do evil. Is it clear that these trials are sent to develop us, not to destroy us? Let's say we joined a gym and employed a professional trainer. To develop our muscles and to strengthen them he will begin to add a little more weight to the bar.

Even though we may not like it we know that no muscle can grow without it being tested and put to great strain. Exercise is not always pleasant but it is always necessary for physical growth and strength. What we are actually doing with our muscle is tearing it down. When we rest the muscle it is given the opportunity to reform and develop larger and stronger, so that it can handle heavier weight.

If our personal trainer added a little more weight to the bar and we begged him to take the weight down every time, it would do us no good. We would never develop the physical strength we needed, and we would stay physical weaklings. It is the same thing spiritually. If every time the enemy came against us and we beg God for deliverance, we are spiritual weaklings.

We have to understand the enemy is going to come against us because we are his enemy. We are living in his world and we are not of this world. We are of the world that is to come. We are not ambassadors of this world any longer. We are ambassadors of the kingdom of heaven. We do not represent Satan any longer, nor do we do the things that bring him glory. We now bring glory and honor to our new Father. We are now establishing God's kingdom.

We have now become the enemy of the god of this world. He is not the only enemy. Along with Satan are his two allies, the world and the flesh. And they will not give you any rest until the day you are promoted into God's kingdom either by death or by the rapture.

These three sworn enemies that are of our faith and are now ours are not going to leave us alone. We have to become strong enough to push them back when they invade our privacy. Young people of today love to call it their space. They love to say you are invading my territory.

When the world, the flesh, and the devil comes into our territory in order to do what they do, we need to be developed spiritually to push them out by overcoming them with the word of God. We cannot get strong or develop spiritual maturity, knowledge and wisdom we need if we don't go through the spiritual testing.

Do you recall what Peter said? Men and brethren count it all joy when you are allowed to be tested. He did not say take it as an opportunity to complain or cry. As difficult to understand as this is we must count it as a joy when we have been found to be worthy to be tested and tried. These minor trials have been sent our way not to disobey but to empower us.

The devil, in his mind, is an awesome opponent. In his diluted mind he is more than the equal of God, he believes he is greater than God. We have to understand his mind is cracked. He is like someone who is hopped up on drugs. He has no understanding or reality of truth.

He is a defeated foe with no power or authority over the believers. Everything he once had has been taken from him. God has crushed his head through the crucifixion of

Christ. Essentially Satan is operating with his head wrapped in a bandage for eternity.

When your head is broken you do not have any power. The devil is running around thinking he is all that, as we sometimes like to say today. Because of his arrogance, the Lord uses Satan against himself.

What was Job's sin? There was no sin that brought him under the attention of the enemy. What brought the attention of the adversary to Job were Job's righteousness and his obedience to God. Job was a thorn in the devil's side. Everyone else was doing their own thing; however, the devil wasn't concerned about them because he already had them under his control. Why go around testing them when they were already under his authority.

He was concerned only with the one he could not control. When Satan went to God and the Lord brought up Job's righteousness, he became angry and sarcastic. The devil replied by saying that Job was this way only because of what God does for him. He asked God to allow him to put Job to the test and then the so-called righteous Job will curse God to His face.

The one thing Job never did was to curse God.
....
Christians are guilty of cursing God when we feel the affliction of the enemy in our lives. Stop it! Stop it! Once we begin to grumble against God, we are grumbling against our only protection. We are grumbling against our shelter, our tabernacle, our protector, our covering, our shield, and

our strength. We are forcing God to do what Israel forced God to do in *Numbers 24.*

By their grumbling much grumbling and complaining, they forced God to judge them.

When we grumble and complain in God's ear we force Him to bring into our lives that which we have complained about in His ear. Be very careful! We bring judgment on ourselves because of what we do and say that is contrary to God's word. Can you understand what I just said? It is so important to grasp this truth otherwise this allows the devil to win and run around bringing confusion into our lives.

Stop the grumbling and complaining at once and say with Job, "Blessed be the Lord my God." Let's remind ourselves to say in the face of adversity, "I know that my redeemer lives and in the last days He shall stand on the face of the earth."

Job didn't even have the Holy Spirit filling him and living within him as we have today. Yet Job had enough understanding to know that his redeemer lived and in the last days would stand on the earth and all the kingdoms of the world would come under His authority and leadership. In spite of the devil's opinion or his effects, the Messiah would come and Satan could not stop Him from becoming the King.

Are we so confident in our spirits that when we are going into trials and testing, we have the knowledge to know where it is coming from? God is not sending the trials and testing your way because He is punishing us and out to destroy us. However, Satan has made it seem that way all because we are his enemy. God is trying to get us to understand that what the enemy meant for evil He is turning it to our good. Satan is trying to tear us down to destroy us and bring us back into bondage.

The very thing the enemy is using against us, God is using to strengthen us and turn us into strong men. And as strong men we can walk on the enemy, not in his weakness but at his stronger time. We are defeating the devil at the height of his power. God is showing us the reality of *Philippians 4:13* – I can do all things, through Christ who strengthens me.

Now one or two things are going to happen when the enemy comes to trouble us because it's nature and his job to do so. Therefore, quit worrying about it when he does those things. Face it; he is not going to act like a saint or like an angel of God. He is going to run around causing havoc and frustration. It's his method of operation, his job code or rather a requirement of what it takes to be a devil. He is a liar, a thief, and a murderer. It's who he is and there is no good in him. For that reason there is no sense in asking him to leave us alone.

He is a bully and the more we ask a bully to leave us alone the more he will torment us. He will oppress us. Let's get about our business, stand up, push him back, and force him away. It's merely a trial God has allowed to happen. Please be clear on this, God did not cause this to happen. He allowed it, not to destroy us but to develop us. He said in the Old Testament, "I know my thoughts toward you, not to harm you but to bless you. Not to destroy you but to help you."

God knows what is needed to help us. He does not want us to be wimps but to be strong warriors and fulfill the image He has of us, not the image we have. Forget the image we have in our minds. This image will fail us and keep us in bondage and limit us.
Thank God He sees us, not as we do, but He sees us in the image He has created us in, which is the image of His Son. If His Son can do all things, then we can as well by His power.

Here is an amazing thought!

You are the tabernacle of God's Spirit, the tabernacle of the Godhead. If Jesus is going to do something on earth, it will be done through His earthly tabernacle His people and that means us. God sees us in the image He created us in. He knows we can overcome any adversity which comes our way. He knows that the god of this world has nothing in us any longer, and God is trying to get that revelation to us. Once we realize who we are, whom we belong to, and what we can do because of the One who is in us, we will stand up face to face with the devil. We will not be afraid of him anymore.

When we conquer the schoolyard bully we are not afraid of him anymore. He is actually afraid of us. When we conquer the devil face to face we will not be afraid of him anymore. When we once and for all truly understand we can do all things through Christ who strengthens us, there is no weapon made or formed that can conquer us. God stops the slanderous tongue, the curse falls to the ground harmlessly, and no one can stop you. God, who created us in the image of His Son, has no desire to stop us from increasing His kingdom, and Satan cannot stop us because all power and authority has been taken from him. It has been taken from him and placed in us.

We can now do all things through Christ; therefore, the only power that can stop us is not the devil's tactics, but it's us because of our unbelief. We make the decision to be stopped. *Philippians 4:13*

Christ gives us the strength to not only endure the tough times, but also to grow during them. We aren't meant to just slog through the pain; we're meant to see our faith blossom right in the face of our battles. God equips us with the armor we need to stand firm:

"Therefore put on the full armor of God, so that when the day of evil comes, you may be able to stand your ground, and after you have done everything, to stand." (*Ephesians 6:13*)

In today's circle of prophecies, many words are given.

Some come from the spirit of God.

Some from the spirit of man.

Some come from counterfeit spirits.

TEST the spirit that speaks to you whether it's from man or from a voice without.

John is speaking to believers. He calls them "beloved." He says we are not to "believe every spirit" but "test" them as to "whether they are of God." Why? Because there are "many false prophets" who have "gone out into the world

1 John 4:2 · Chapter 4 · 1 John 3:24

Did Jesus Christ come in the flesh and is he coming again?

CHAPTER 11

.....Satan's Ability to Hinder Our Calling.....

It is the devil's intention to afflict the righteous and hinder us or stop us from fulfilling the call in our lives. Satan is working to take our salvation away from us or get us to denounce our citizenship in heaven. He wants to stop us from being the ambassadors of the kingdom of heaven and from realizing that we are sons or daughters of the living God.

We have been recreated from what we were yesterday into what we are today. We have been created in the image of Jesus Christ Himself. If the devil cannot do all of these things, then he will try to steal or hinder the call in our lives because if we do what we have been commissioned to do, we will tear down his kingdom. It is simple. If you obey God then go forth in the strength of Him and His Spirit.

People fear demon-possessed people. They will say, "Oh the power this person has!" No, that person is filled with the power of Satan. So what! We are filled with the power of God. If I have my choice of strength, it definitely isn't the strength of the devil. It is nothing compared to the unlimited power of the God of Creation.

The strength of God is within us; even scripture says we have the strength of God. We also have the mind of Christ and the power of the Holy Spirit in us. We are covered in the blood of the Lamb. What more do we need to be successful? What more do we honestly need to be victorious? God has anointed every believer. All we have to do is let go of self, and then more of God will be exposed through us.

We must understand who we are in Christ, and then we will obey the Father. As we obey Him we will go forth and establish His kingdom. Thy kingdom come Thy will be done here on earth. How it is done in heaven? As we **go forth** we establish the kingdom of heaven.

As we develop the kingdom of heaven we are tearing down the kingdom of darkness. Push back the kingdom of Satan and destroy it! Take back from the devil that which he stole from our fathers. God is going to back us up one hundred percent.

For instance, it's like a king who has a warrior that comes to him and says, "Oh king, you have an enemy who stole from you and with your permission I would like to go forth in your name and authority to take back that which your enemy has stolen from you." We know the king will back him up one hundred percent. This means all the wealth and authority of that king and his kingdom will be behind that warrior. As the king's representative all the ground he recovers will mean the kingdom will be expanded, How could the king not give his full support?

When we **go forth** in the name of Christ conquering the kingdom of darkness, God's kingdom is expanded. Guess what? The fullness of the glory of heaven and the kingdom of God is backing us in this battle. Go forth and take back what belongs to God. Trust me, He will back us.

Every soul that dies and goes to hell is a soul paid for by the blood of Christ. It is a soul stolen from God by the enemy. Does God want that soul? He wants it more than we want it. He needs people to go forth to rescue those who are perishing. God is not going to hinder us neither will He allow a defeated soul to stop us.

In order to become soldiers we need to be trained and we need to be tested. **Need to be disciplined. Why?** It is to prove that we won't run once we get into the battle. That is all that God is doing when He is allows Satan to test us. It simply proves to us and to the enemy what we will do in the midst of the battle.

God already knows what we will do. We just need to be convinced that we will stand and that we will do all we can to stand. We must stand with our loins girt with truth, and the enemy must be taught that we are not going to be pushed around. He is not going to know that unless he comes up against us.

If we run, then he knows he can torment us. If we don't run and we fight back, he is going to have to consider whether or not the price is worth it. Chances are he is not going to be willing to pay the price over and over again.

"Consider it pure joy, my brothers, whenever you face trials of many kinds, because you know that the testing of your faith develops perseverance. Perseverance must finish its work so that you may be mature and complete, not lacking anything." (*James 1:2–4*)

CHAPTER 12

.....Satan's Ability to Affect the Sinner.....

It is Satan's job to keep the sinner in bondage, and under his domain. He is going to keep him prisoner and under his command. The devil is like a pit bull. He will not let go until a stronger power makes him let go and with force. Pray to the Father that the enemy can never take it back.

The Bible tells us if we want to enter the strongman's house we must first bind the strongman. Once we have bound the strongman, we can freely enter his house and do whatsoever we want to do, because we will have no oppression. We bind the enemy through prayer. If the enemy has someone in his authority, he will do everything in his power to keep him until a stronger one than himself comes and delivers that person.

In *Acts 16:16-18* we find the story of a young girl, who is said in the King James Version to be a young damsel, possessed by a fortune telling spirit. In the Greek it says the spirit of the python possessed her. The python is the king of snakes. Now the Bible calls the devil, that old serpent so it shows us in the Greek the nature of the spirit in that young girl.

It was more than just a fortune-teller and more than a gypsy who read by leaves. It was the full power of the king of serpents, the devil. A strongman, not just a simple demon or an imp, but a power of a wicked spirit and a principality in high places possessed her. Her earthly masters to bring great wealth to them were using her. What happened when she was set free?

Everyone went crazy because that one girl being set free brought down the financial security of the local economy, and Paul ended up in prison. God used even that to being salvation to the jailer and his entire family.

From this we understand that no matter what the enemy is going to do to us in opposition of what God is doing in your life, God will turn it around to our benefit. Every curse directed at us, God is going to turn it into a blessing. If we can realize this we will never doubt God. We will never grumble against God. We will never bring a negative accusation against Him of things He is not guilty of.

It is just as we mentioned before about 'acts of God'. The world takes what is happening and blames God for it. God is innocent. Yet the world does not understand God and sees Him as some kind of awesome power who gets angry and sends torment. Therefore, they blame God for what the enemy is responsible for, calling every act or massive act of destruction an act of God.

It's as if God has to throw a fit every once in a while. That is not our God. It is the god of this world. Our God does not have to do this. God does not need to bring destruction in our lives to get our attention. He can do it by lifting things up. God will turn around every negative act of the enemy. If the enemy throws a rock at you, by the time it gets to you it will be turned into a flower. God will turn every negative action into something positive, if you will let Him. Quit accusing Him and just let Him have His way in our lives without complaint.

Remember if God is for us, who can stand against us? If God is fighting this battle for us how can we lose this battle? We can say a lot of popular things as Christians. And that is one of the reasons why I don't like to use notes when I preach. I like to be free to feel the Spirit.

If we truly believe in the catchy phrases we say as believers then we would get a lot more done. The evidence of the Spirit of God would be more real in our lives. Everywhere we go in this world, we would change it for God. We would be in total agreement with ourselves. We struggle to come in agreement with our brothers and sisters to get things done when we can't come in agreement with ourselves.

With our heart we believe unto righteousness and with our mouth we make confession to salvation. We can't even get our hearts and tongues to agree. Never mind coming in agreement with anyone else. Once we come into agreement with ourselves it will be easy to come into agreement with others, and great and wonderful things will happen. We will be able to rescue the sinners from the hands of a crude master.

The harder he tries to keep them, the more we will resist him, and the harder we will try to bring the captives out. The church has been commissioned by God to go through the entire world and preach the gospel and to make disciples of all nations. And a simple scripture, I love, says that the gates of hell shall not prevail against the church of God.

I am sure you're wondering what does all this have to do with keeping sinners under the domain of Satan? The best way to keep a person under your authority is to place them in a prison. The greatest prison ever is hell. The kingdom of hell on the earth is the kingdom of Satan.

As it is in heaven, let it be here on earth. We are trying to bring God's kingdom down here on earth, but the enemy is also trying to turn the kingdom of the earth into the kingdom of hell on earth. He is trying to bring the fullness of hell right here on earth. He is trying to make earthly life into a hellish life. It is darkness, despair, bondage, and imprisonment.

This is what he does with those under his ruler ship; he enslaves them one way or another through false religions. He also does this through alcohol, narcotics, emotion and depression, physical problems, and infirmity. He uses anything and everything he can to put people in bondage. He is busy spreading hell by his people here on earth but the Bible says that the gates of hell shall not prevail against the believers.

What does this mean; gates don't move backwards or forwards? Gates are stationary. They stay in one place. It means that the church of Christ is marching toward the gates of hell. What's the purpose? They are marching to set the captives free and to bring them out from under the authority and in bondage to the enemy.

Isaiah 42 says there are those who are in caves, in holes in the grounds, and in prisons who need restored but no one delivers them. There are those who have been taken into captivity by the god of this world. These captives are the trophies of Satan – the trophies of hell itself. God desires these people to be restored. His Son has given His life to restore them, to bring them redemption to bring them freedom, to bring them salvation, and to bring them joy and peace. However, they are in dark places, in spiritual caves, spiritual holes in the ground, and spiritual prisons. No one is going to them and saying to him or her – be restored, be redeemed. It is time for the church to do it.

Over and over again the scripture speaks about God looking everywhere for a man who would be willing to stand in the gap. Why? Do we stand in the gap so we can complain to God about the faults of our brothers and sisters? No! He is looking for someone who is willing to lay his life down. No greater love has a man than the one who would sacrifice his life for his brother.

No greater love has man or women of God than to be willing to stand in the gap as an intercessor for the salvation of those in bondage. We are to pray for the redemption of our enemies, love those who hate us, pray for those who persecute us, and bless those who curse us. Scripture hasn't changed. This is what the church of Christ should be doing.

If we are doing it, then those who are in bondage to a lie will run to us by the thousands to be saved for they will see the truth being manifested through us. It won't be just a written truth, but a living truth that brings freedom and light wherever it goes. This is what we are meant to be. We can help to set these captives free.

Satan keeps these people under his domain, but have you ever noticed that when you speak to these people they have no understanding? Their minds are clogged and they are not clear on anything. No matter how intelligent they proclaim to be, the simplest things of the Spirit confuse, frustrate, and anger them. Why? It's without a doubt one of the strongholds of the enemy. One of his functions is to bind the minds of the unbelievers by keeping them in confusion.

When I was involved in the occult years ago I could teach men anything I wanted to teach them, and make them believe every word I said. I could make what I said to look spiritual. I could tell them the tree was their master, and I could get someone to actually bow down and worship that tree. No matter how educated they were or what their position was in life, I could convince them that the tree was to be worshipped and they would worship that tree.

I could tell them anything I wanted to tell them about the occult world and they would believe it. I could tell them I could read their minds and they would believe I could read their minds. I could tell them I could read the lines on their palms and they would believe I could. There was nothing that I would say to them that sounded religious that they would not believe except if I told them the truth.

I could tell these people who did not know Christ anything, whether they were man or woman, they would believe it. I could teach them anything I wanted to as long as I didn't mention Jesus. However, once I begin to tell them about Jesus and the truth of His word, they could not understand it. They would look at me as if I lost my mind.

When I used to tell people I was a witch, and I could do this and I could do that, they thought I was an intelligent human being. I was someone they wanted to be around. They wanted to follow me, because they wanted to be like me.

Then God reached down into all that foolishness and darkness, and delivered me, set me free, and filled me with His Holy Spirit. When I began to tell these same people about Jesus Christ, they would look at me as if I had lost my mind, as if I went crazy. My wife's parents turned their back on us. My own father turned his back on us. According to them we were nuts because we were talking about Jesus and the Bible.

Why was that? Why was it that they were willing to listen to me when I taught lies, but when I taught truth they wouldn't listen? It was because the enemy had bound their minds. He binds the minds of the people of this world, which is the way Satan keeps them in bondage and continuing down the path of destruction.

He gives them false light and the only hope they have is that someone like us, who are born again and spiritually mature will bring the light of the word to them and set them free. We need to bind the strongman when we approach a person who does not know Jesus. Please do not take witnessing lightly.

We need intercessors and evangelists.

I mean street evangelists, not people who want to stand behind the pulpit and talk to thousands of people. Doing that is wonderful and a true ministry calling, but we need people who are willing to go to the streets, to the market places, and to everyone they meet in their daily lives and bring the message of salvation to them.

We need people who are willing to support these evangelistic people in prayer so they are covered because the strongman over their lives of the people they minister needs to be bound. There is a demonic spirit assigned to each and every person on the earth. Their assignment is to keep these people in bondage and to keep them from the truth of the word. They take their assignment very seriously and they do it with everything within them.

They do not want you taking what they have stolen from our heavenly Father from them. If you do rescue that person, they will have to give an account to their master. They do not want to face the devil, because they have no protection against him or his wrath. Praise God we do! We need to understand that if we truly hate the devil and his demons as much as we say we do, then we will take great joy in causing them aggravation and headache.

We would do everything we could to take from the jaw of the lion the lamb he has just stolen. Like David we wouldn't fear the lion. Neither did David fear the bear or the giant. David knew his God and a lion was just a lion, a bear was just a bear, and the giant was only a giant. What were these three compared to his God who created everything?

They were nothing. David had the confidence that not only did his God hear his prayer, but that His God also responded to it. He answered David and delivered him from any enemy that came against him, or came his way.

We need to be like that. We need to look at these tormenting spirits and say what are they. Of course there are those who will say, "Oh they're demons, brother. They might be fallen angels, principalities, and wicked spirits in high places, powers, and strongmen. Oh we don't have any rights against them."

I beg to differ. The Bible says that anything which exalts itself against God or puffs itself up against Christ; we have the authority and power to cast it down. Start using the authority God has given to us. We must realize we are the strongman that God has chosen to replace the old strongman. He wants you to come in and conquer the king, the ruler of that area, and a cast him down.

Once a king conquers another king he becomes ruler in his place and everything the former king had now becomes the property of the new king. We now become the strongman over the area. It is our job now to keep the previous strongman out. We need intercessors to pray that the strongman is bound over the life of the unbeliever.

At the beginning of our day, before we do anything or before we go anywhere, we must go to our heavenly Father in the name of Jesus Christ His beloved Son. We should say, *"Father, wherever we go today we ask Lord that what we bind on earth, You will bind in heaven. We bind the strongman over the life of every person we may come into contact with so that he can no longer keep this person in bondage and captivity. Satan can no longer keep them away from You oh Lord. This is the day of salvation for every person we come into contact with so we bind these spirits here on earth knowing You will bind them in the high places so that they can no longer keep the people from You. Therefore, Father as we bind them here on earth, may You bind them in the heavens. We loose your Spirit on the earth as You loose it in the heavens. We ask that You send Your angels to minister to this person. If we loose it here on earth, we know You will loose it in the heavens. Victory will be Yours today and souls will be added to Your kingdom."*

As we do this we will see the increase of God's kingdom. We will see these people who once looked at us in discontent, bitterness, hate, and confusion and see understanding and joy come into their eyes. Why? Because the imp that held their eyes closed and kept their mind confused has been bound and cannot interfere any longer. He has been cast aside.

Now the new strongman has come into the territory of the old strongman which we have bound. Now we can do what we want to do because his territory has become God's, and he cannot come against us any longer and interfere against us.

Is this clear? Do you understand this is what run to the battle is? This is spiritual warfare. It is battling against spirits, not against man.

It is taking the Spirit of God wherever you go and casting down the spirit of the antichrist or the spirit of Lucifer.

It is bringing everything into captivity to the Holy Spirit of the living God, and setting the captives free by the authority in the word, and the name of Jesus and the blood of the lamb. Amen.

Casting down imaginations, and every high thing that exalteth itself against the knowledge of God, and bringing into captivity every thought to the obedience of Christ
2 Corinthians 10:5

CHAPTER 13

.....The Weapon of the Word of God.....

I want to reiterate what **Ephesians 6:12** says, 'For WE wrestle not against flesh and blood but against spirits'. We wrestle not against flesh and blood. We need to grasp this truth. No man is our enemy. We have only one enemy and that is Satan. Our fight and battle is against spiritual wickedness, power and authority in the high places. The devil contends and wars against us.

In the early 19th century *Jessie Penn-Lewis wrote War On The Saints* and tried to portray the battle between the kingdom of Satan and the saints of God. She showed how the enemy came against the saints; how he infected them, how he impaired them, and how he did everything he could to stop them from increasing the kingdom of God.

One of the best weapons the enemy has to stop us dead in our tracks is to take away the knowledge of the word of God. If we start our morning on a pop tart and a cup of coffee, by the afternoon we are going to run out of steam. We need a good breakfast in order to fuel our bodies to operate and function properly. If we put junk in we're going to get junk out. We need to put something of value in high octane so our engines keep running smoothly.

If we start our day on our daily verse of scripture we pluck out of our scripture box like a fortune cookie, it is not going to give us the strength we need to come against the enemy. We need the word of God. We need to put the word in us before we go to bed. We need to put the word in us as soon as we wake up. We need to be dreaming about the word while we are lying in bed sleeping. The enemy will even try to invade our sleep through our dreams. We should be so full of the word that even as we are sleeping the word of God is coming out of us and we stop him.

We need to be so filled with the word of God that every time the enemy squeezes us, all that oozes out is God's word. It is written Satan, it is written. It shouldn't be, words like: I feel, maybe, or perhaps. It should come out in the power that only the word can come out in.

An opinion of the word is weak. The word is a powerful double-edged sword and it does powerful things in the battle because it cuts both ways. We don't need to worry about wielding a double-edged sword because when we are swinging this thing back and forth and we hit the enemy, he will feel the cutting blow.

The word will wound him. Our **opinion** of the word is not even a good jack knife. We do not go into battle with a jack knife. We go to battle with the weapons of warfare, which is the sword. The sword pushes the enemy from us when he comes at us with his limited weapons.

Oh yes, the enemy has limited weapons. It's the same old weapons time and time again; however, his strength lies with his familiarity of the weapon. He knows how to use them and how to use them against us.

We have unlimited resources at our disposal. We have sixty-six books of the Bible called the word of God. They are our sword, our shield, our buckler, our breastplate, our helmet, and our shoes, so use them. They are our strong tower, our Sabbath, our rest, our strength, our weapons, and our hiding place. They sustain us by being our meat to our spirit and our bread of life from above.

Because the word is the source that nourishes and strengthens us, it enables us to fight back against the enemy. Not only do we fight back but the word also helps us to push the enemy back and drive him out. The scripture says the enemy may come at you one way but he will flee from you in seven different ways. Amen.

We must know who we are in Christ and the nature that is ours. Do we understand the tools God has given us? I'm not talking about commentaries or books that have an opinion. I am talking about the **word of God**. When we understand it and it becomes such a part of us that it comes out every time we open our mouth then the enemy cannot stand against us. He must flee from us.

We must be familiar with our weapons. We have to know how that sword feels in our hand and what it can do. We must know how the shield works and it become a part of our arm. As we move our arm the shield moves with us. It is not an artificial thing.

For instance, years ago when I was in the martial arts, the very beginning of my training was thinking of every movement I was going to do. As I progressed and finally received my black belt, I no longer had to think about these movements, they were so natural that they had become a part of me. I moved before I even thought about it. It was as natural as breathing.

The word of God has to become that way. The word has to be coming out of us even before the attack. The word should now be our nature. It is how we now function. When a man curses us, we bless him. The old man or the old nature would have cursed him back. We are even surprised and may say, "Where did that come from?" It came from your new nature.

It came from our spirit which has been recreated in the image of our Father. Therefore we no longer fight in the ways of our old father, the devil. We now fight this battle in the image of our new Father. We no longer have the weapons of our old father, which are the lies, the curses, the insults, the gossip, and the false accusations. We now have our new Father's weapons: we bless, we edify, we lift up, we exalt, and we establish. We cannot help ourselves because it is a part of us, and we do it before we realize what we're doing. Amen.

CHAPTER 14

.....A Weapon of the Enemy.....

The next weapon of the enemy is found in *Hebrews 2:14* which is to inspire lying wonders and false miracles. My wife wants me to do a series called lying wonders and miracles because every wonder and miracle that happens is not always from God.

Satan can appear as an angel of light and can do good things. However, he doesn't like to do good things and he won't do it unless there is a purpose that is going to benefit him. Every miracle you see does not mean it is from God. Consider the difference between the miracles of Jehovah God and the gods of Egypt. When God did His miracles the false gods of Egypt copied some of the miracles of God. Did that make them true gods and righteous? No, it made them counterfeit.

All signs, wonders and miracles going on aren't necessarily from God. It may be the enemy working to keep people deceived and in bondage. In Onset, Massachusetts when my wife and I first got saved, we attended a little Pentecostal church, which was an Assembly of God church.

Right next door to this Spirit-filled church was a spiritual church founded on the teaching of the Fox sisters on spiritualism. Every Friday for two miles on both sides of the road there were cars parked full of people who went to that church. Many of them received false miracles. The blind eyes see, the deaf hear, the dumb spoke and the lame walked. All this was done by a deceiving spirit and not by God.

Now many will ask, "How can Satan heal or open the eyes of the blind or cause the lame to walk?" Know this for certain, Satan is NOT Jehovah God. Know this as well, if Satan can put this on a person, he can take it off. He will do false miracles to increase his kingdom and to keep people in bondage. Therefore do not be deceived by every miracle or signs and wonders. I have seen demon-possessed people speak in tongues. I have seen the gift of the Spirit counterfeited, but I have never seen the fruits of the Spirit imitated.

I am Pentecostal and I firmly believe in the gifts of the Spirit. I thank God for the gifts, but I do not base my maturity on the gift. I base it on the fruits of the spirit. We do not need to be mature to have the gifts; however, we cannot have the fruits of God's Spirit and be immature. Remember God used a donkey in the Old Testament to prophesy to the prophet but He didn't give to him the fruit of patience and long suffering.

In previous chapters we have discussed who Satan is and how he works in the lives of the believer and the unbeliever. We also examined how he functions in the lives of people like blinding the unbelievers to the truth. His plans are to destroy them.

We studied how he contends and wars against the saints of God. We get a little confused and think to ourselves, if he is so powerful and seems to be everywhere what can we do against him? What chance do we have against him? Compared to God, Satan is the complete opposite. Where God is righteous and pure, Satan is corrupt and polluted God is all knowing and is everywhere while Satan is limited in his knowledge and cannot be everywhere.

The Scriptures tell us if I descend to hell, and make my bed there You (God) are there. If I go to the deepest part of the sea You are there. If I ascend to the highest height of heaven You are there. Where can we escape God's spirit? The answer is nowhere.
He gave them the rights to serve Him or they could refuse. We know Lucifer allowed pride to manifest in his life. He turned his back on his loving Creator. Lucifer wasn't any different than the other angels. He was a created being just like Michael, Gabriel, and thousands of other angels whose names we do not know.

The same God who made us created the angels. They were created with more power, might, and understanding than we are, for a season. There will come a time when we will judge angels. We will become greater than the angels. No angels were formed in the image of God and reborn into the reflection of Christ Jesus. Only man, who the scriptures says was created in God's image, will rule and reign with Christ. We will be directly under the Trinity.

The angels will be under us, and we need to understand that angels like man can be in only one place at a time. Even though Satan is a great adversary, he can only be in one place at a time. Do not deceive yourself or fool yourself into believing he is not a powerful enemy. He is the greatest force in creation outside of the Trinity.

If it was not for the blood of Jesus, the word of God, the name of Jesus, and the Holy Spirit of the living God, we, as created beings, would not stand a chance against him. We don't need to delude ourselves and become arrogant. Neither should we misconstrue the point I am trying to get across. It is true that the devil is a defeated foe; however, he was defeated but NOT by us. He was defeated on the cross of Calvary by Jesus Christ.

Over two thousand years ago God's Son took Satan's power and authority from him and all authority in heaven and earth was given to Jesus. And Jesus gave all power and authority to us. He gave us the ability to tread on scorpions and serpents. He gave us power over the enemy. He made you the head and not the tail. He placed you above the enemy. He placed Satan under you. Warning! Do not become arrogant or prideful or think that we are a force to be reckoned with outside of Jesus.

Outside of Jesus we would be consumed quicker than we could bat our eyes. The most significant aspect of spiritual warfare is understanding who God is and how awesome He is.

CHAPTER 15

.....Jehovah God – Our Creator, Our Father.....

God, our Creator, is so vast that heaven is His throne and the earth is His footstool.(*Isaiah 66:1*) God looks down upon the earth and sees it as a footstool. Amazing! We are a minor creation compared to God.

Since we have been covered by the blood of Jesus and ransomed because of His sacrifice, do we completely comprehend who our new Father is? It is imperative that we know His power, because we are now joint heirs with the Lord. We are ruling and reigning with Christ and we are sitting in high places with Him. We are ambassadors of the kingdom of God on the earth. *(2 Corinthians 5:20)*

We represent our Father and everywhere we go people understand our Father by understanding us. They come to realize the nature and attributes of our Father because they see the same nature and attributes in us.

While growing up, my earthly father forged my personality, my character and my habits by exposing me to the way he handled life. The way my father dealt with situations became the way I handle them. His personality, his attributes, his strengths, and his weaknesses were manifested through me as his son.

No matter where I went, people saw a reflection of my earthly father. Most would say, "Wow! We can sure see that your Mickey's son. You look just like him. You walk like him and you talk like him. You act like him too because you respond to things just like he does."

They knew I was my father's son and not his brother's because I didn't have my uncle's character. Since my father was well known in the city people would not even ask me my name whenever I happened to come around. They simply watched how I did things and they just associate me with my father. Do you understand what I am saying?

If we are a mirror image of our earthly father, so should it be with our heavenly Father. Everywhere we go people should see His love and compassion reflected through us. God's ways become ours because we study our heavenly Father. (*Hebrews 1: 1-4*)

We do not study the devil or his ways unless God directs us to. If He does, then He will lead us because there is a purpose that He has for this. For instance the Lord may want us to become teachers of world religions and cults. This should only happen if He directs us down this path. We should not knowingly go on our own. If He leads us then we will be covered and protected by Him.

He will show us what He wants us to see. Understand, he doesn't want us to study the devil in the context of becoming terrified by him or to teach how powerful Satan is. God wants us to see him as he is and that he exists and he is real. BUT…he is *limited*!

God wants us to study about Him. He wants us to know all there is to know about our heavenly Father and His word. He wants us to know the truth because by knowing the truth we will never be deceived by the counterfeit.

It is solid truth that will get us through every trial which comes our way. Frankly I don't appreciate pastors or preachers that tell people by becoming born again they won't face trials. The truth is when we become born again we will face more trials than we have before.

It is because we have come from the kingdom of darkness to the kingdom of God and His Christ. *Colossians 1:13*

 We went from a kingdom where we were slaves to God's kingdom where we are sons or daughters to Him.

We are joint heirs with Christ.(*Romans 8:17*) We went from slavery to kingship and a ruler ship in God's kingdom.

We are now priests and prophets. (*1 Peter 2:9*)

We are new creatures remade into the image of Christ. (*2 Corinthians 5:17*)

Therefore, if anyone is in Christ, the new creation
has come: The old has gone, the new is here!
2 Corinthians 5:17

CHAPTER 16

.....God is Victorious Over the Enemy's Schemes.....

Be sober, be vigilant; because your adversary the devil, as a roaring lion, walketh about, seeking whom he may devour: whom resist steadfast in the faith, knowing that the same afflictions are accomplished in your brethren that are in the world" (1 Peter 5:8-9).

The devil is certainly real but what are his plans and how is he scheming to destroy us? He intends to steal our children, ruin our marriages, destroy our jobs, take our finances, and ruin our relationship with people we come in contact with as well as God. He wants to take our health and peace of mind. He will hinder us from living for God in any way he can. *(2 Timothy 1:7)*

He steals our joy because if he can do that, he can steal our strength. Scripture says the joy of the Lord is our strength and our salvation. I shared with my wife recently that the joy of teaching was just recently taken from me. When the joy of teaching was taken from me, I was teaching from a weakness or limitation. There was no power, no authority, and no anointing on my teaching. Why? My joy, which was my strength, was gone.

When the joy of teaching returned, the strength returned and the anointing returned. Who stole the joy of teaching from me? It wasn't God. The enemy used situations in my life like oppositions, grumbling, complaining, slander, defamation of character, and lies to stop the joy of teaching God's word. It was like who cares. Every time I had to stand to teach the word I had to face all of this. I began to get depressed and began to lose that joy. This is how the enemy works in our lives.

We do NOT teach about Satan to glorify him, to give him any honor, nor to make him any larger than he is. We do not want to make any kind of evil equal with God. He most definitely is not. Many people in main line denominations portray Satan as being so powerful that it looks like they were in a celestial arm wrestling competition and it depended on man. Who would be determined the winner?

If Satan is so powerful what chance do we have against him? He seems to be everywhere. God is righteous, holy and pure and he seems to be the evil opposite. God is everywhere, not the devil. The psalmist says if I ascend to heaven You (God) are there, then if I go to the bottom of the sea You are there. If I descend to the lowest hell You are there. Where can I hide myself from You? Basically the psalmist is telling God that no matter where we go, Lord, Your Spirit is always there.

Even though Satan is not everywhere, his influence is. He is like us. He can only be in one place at a time. Is he like God? NO! He is an evil being who has power but he is not all-powerful.

Before the physical world and the realm we call reality, God created the sons of God known as angels. They were righteous, holy, and pure. And God, being a fair God, gave to them the gift of free will as he did for man. Just like He gave to man, He gave the angels the decision to serve Him willingly or not to serve Him. Lucifer allowed pride to enter in him and he turned his back on his loving Creator.

Lucifer is a **created** being, just like Michael and Gabriel and thousands upon thousands of other angels. The same God that created us created them. They were created to be great in power and might and understanding, but only for a season. There will come a time that we will judge them and be greater in power.

We will be greater because only man was created in the image of Christ and only man by the help of God can understand salvation. It is amazing that only man, God's greatest creation, is made in the image of our Lord Jesus Christ. We will be directly under the Trinity and the angels will be directly under us.

Now we must remember no matter how strong an angel is, like man, he can be only one place at a time. That means Satan can only be at one place at a time. Satan is a great adversary and a most powerful force there is besides the Trinity. If it wasn't for the blood of Jesus and the Holy Spirit we would be defeated easily. Therefore, we do not need to deceive ourselves, nor do we need to become arrogant.

It's true the devil is a defeated adversary. We cannot be conceited to think we have anything to do with it. It was Christ in the desert and on the cross of Calvary that defeated Satan, not us. However God has given the same power and authority given to Jesus to us. He has placed the enemy under our feet and we are over his head. Do not make the mistake and think we are a force to be reckoned with.

God is so vast and earlier I spoke of the scripture that says He looks down on the earth as His footstool. We are so small compare to our awesome God. We have now been redeemed by the blood of Jesus and changed into the image of the second Adam, Christ. We are new creatures with a marvelous new heavenly Father.

We are joint heirs with Jesus (*Romans 8:17*) all that He has is ours. We rule and reign with Him. We are sitting with Him right now in heavenly places. As ambassadors for the kingdom of God, all of the military power of God and all of the wealth of the kingdom is ours. Our Father in heaven has given them to us. Everything Jesus did we can do and greater so that our Father's kingdom can be expanded here on earth.

We have been chosen to represent our Father. Wherever we go people see our Father in us. We have His eyes, we talk like Him, we walk like Him, and we copy every thing we see Him do and that we hear Him say. People will understand the nature and attributes of our Father as we allow them to be manifest through us.

When I first came to the Lord there was a teaching going on telling us that we were not worthy of salvation. It proclaimed we were lower than the belly of a worm. The belly of a worm touches the dirt so how low can we go. If we were below the belly of a worm we actually had no value whatsoever.

According to that teaching we were useless and had no value whatsoever. Then there are some of the songs we used to sing that totally depressed, even today, and I wonder why I didn't have any desire to go to church. I mean praying for pennies from heaven. I do not want pennies from heaven. I want the full blessing of heaven in my life. I want the anointing from heaven. I want the power from heaven and the authority. I want the Word of God functioning in my life. I want it fully functioning in my life the way that God wanted it to.

I want the blessing in my life that God wants in my life. I want everything that God wants to give me. I want to be what God wants me to be. I want to do everything that God wants me to do. I want no limitation in my life. For goodness sake, I do not want pennies. I want the fullness of the blessings in my life and my family's lives.

For the longest time we were told that we were **just sinners** saved by grace. No, we **WERE** sinners. The key word is, were. We were in bondage to the god of this world. We were slaves to Pharaoh so to say. Secondly, God delivered us and saved us by His grace, not through our own works lest any man should boast.

We were saved by grace. We were sinners who were saved by the grace of God. Then we were transformed from the old, which passed away, and all things became new. We were transformed from this image we used to be and then transformed into the image of Christ.

We have no concept of what the born again believer is going to look like when we are raptured into the presence of God, as Christ is now so shall we be. We are new creatures and nothing of the old lingers in us unless we bring it across ourselves, and if we are bringing all this with u, then we cannot be truly born again.

If we are still living in yesterday, or if we are still walking around with the corpse of the sinner draped over our shoulders, or if we are carrying the old smelly man who should have been buried and forgotten about, or if we are carrying him everywhere as some kind of a trophy or testimony, then we are not truly free. Yes, at one time I was involved in the occult, a male witch, and I did terrible and stupid things, but I don't know that man any longer. When I stand up to give my testimony and begin to talk about that man of yesterday, I don't know him any better than you know him.

Why? He does not exist any longer. Do you realize that God sits in heaven and wonders who I am talking? In God's mind that old man, that old foolish slave of Satan and this world does not exist any longer. I am a new man. I am a son of God by adoption. When I enter into the courts to praise God and glorify His name, Jesus does not introduce me in this way – "Father, here is Henry Lewis.

He is an ex-witch and the man who did this and the man who did that.

Jesus doesn't do that! He says – "Father, here is my brother and Your adopted son. You bought him by the blood Your child. He is here to worship you." God looks at me, and do you know what he sees? Now this is where a lot of people have a problem. When God looks at me He sees the reflection of His Son. He sees Jesus because the blood of Christ covers me and the spirit of Christ fills me, and I am in the image of His Son, Jesus. He doesn't remind me of my foolishness of yesterday.

Listen, the devil will remind me and man does it all the time, but God never reminds me of that. God tells me of the great and wonderful things that are going to happen in my life. He reminds me that He has redeemed me for a purpose. He doesn't constantly keep bringing me back to yesterday gets me to go forward by the strength of His Spirit and the knowledge of His word.

He wants to do great and wonderful things and to bring me from mountaintop to mountaintop, from high places to high places. *2 Samuel 7:21* Sure there are valleys. We know when we go from one mountaintop to another there are valleys in-between. The valley is low compared to the peak of the mountain, but the valley is not as low as the valley we used to be in. The next valley is still higher than the valley we just came from. We are not regressing we are going forward.

Everything in your life is bringing you onward. We are dynamo for Christ and the Spirit of the living God is within us. We need to know who we are and who lives within us. We are not God and we are not becoming a god. We are not Jesus and we are not becoming Jesus. Guess what? The triune God lives within us, and the kingdom of heaven is within us.

Whenever I ask someone where the kingdom of heaven is, especially a little child, he or she instantly looks to the sky and points beyond the Milky Way and says, "The kingdom of heaven is out there somewhere, Brother Lewis." Jesus said the kingdom of heaven is within. He said if we believe Him and we believe His words, if we abide in Him and He abides in us then His Father and He shall come and establish their kingdom in our hearts.

He said, "I will send you another comforter." Who is this other comforter? It's the Holy Spirit. Where does the Holy Spirit come to dwell? He dwells within us, the tabernacle of clay called man. The kingdom of God abides within us. We are an awesome creation of God, and we need to realize this. We are not lower than the belly of a worm.

Before I was saved I was lower than the belly of a worm, but now I am a prince, a priest, and a prophet. I am of a royal nation, a holy nation, and a peculiar person. We all are if we are believers. We are sons and daughters of God who have been redeemed. The strength of God is within us, and the mind of Christ is within us.

Our tongue within our mouth, according to Proverbs, has the power of life and death. ***Proverbs 18:21*** We either build up or tear down, and we either bind or loose. Whatever we speak in faith can come to pass. In the book of *Numbers* in the Old Testament, God said, "Tell these stiff-necked, hard-hearted, rebellious people whatsoever they speak in my ears I shall cause to come to pass." In the New Testament, God said, "Whatsoever they ask in my Son's name I will bring to pass."

We have power over death, hell, and the grave.(*Revelation 1:18*) We have power over infirmity and we have power over Satan, demons, principalities, and fallen angels.(*Ephesians 1:21,Matthew 10:1,*) We have power because of **who** lives within us because we have been made complete (*Colossians 2:10*). We are more than a worm. We are worth much because of the divine nature within us. Do you understand what I am saying? We should rejoice over what God has done in our lives.

It's like an old vehicle in the junkyard. The engine is dead, the transmission is gone, and the body is rusting away. Then someone comes and takes that old worthless vehicle and with loving-kindness begins to restore it. He takes out the old engine (the old nature) and the old transmission. The engine is driving force or power of the vehicle but the transmission gives the ability to go forward or backward.

Once the mechanic takes out the old engine and the old transmission he lovingly repairs the old body and gives it a new coat of paint. Then he replaces everything within the interior of the vehicle. Basically he turns the old relic into a brand new vehicle any owner would take pride in.

Does that vehicle go around remembering that it was a piece of junk just rotting away on the heap on the junk pile? No, it goes around doing what the mechanic, who restored it, wants it to do. It operates smoothly with the new engine and transmission the mechanic has placed within it.

We were like that old jalopy on the junk pile (Gehenna), but God (our mechanic) secured us just like that old wreck of a vehicle. He lovingly restored us, not in our old nature of the first Adam, but with a new nature of His Son, Jesus. We are now like that vehicle the master mechanic can be proud of. We are to be used for His glory and for His honor, as long as we believe we are new creatures in Christ. When we begin to doubt, we begin to remember what we used to be.

When we listen to the lies of Satan like the one that says we are lower than the belly of a worm or we are useless, or we are just sinners saved by grace or we have to beg for pennies from heaven and we begin to doubt the wonderful redemptive work that God has done in us through the sacrifice of His Son, then we become a vehicle of dishonor. God says that we are His children bought by the shed blood of His Son. He has called us to be ambassadors of His kingdom. He trusts us so much that He allows us to represent Him on the earth.

God said, "I give to you authority and power.

Bring the whole tithe into the storehouse, that there may be food in my house. Test me in this," says the LORD Almighty, "and see if I will not throw open the floodgates of heaven and pour out so much blessing that there will not be room enough to store it (***Malachi 3:10***) The Lord also tells us that He has placed us in the heavenly places with His Son far above any of our enemies. According to the word of God this is taking place right now not when we die, but right at this moment of time we are already sitting there.

The fullness of God's authority, power, and might backs us.(***Colossians 2:10***) Then after all this we turn to God and say, "Well we are nobodies, we are just old sinners saved by grace. Oh Lord, Oh Lord, please send us some pennies from heaven. this is a lowly mentality. Oh Father, just give us the ability to endure, just to endure."

God says, "No! No, that is not why I made you. That is not why I renewed you in the image of My Son." It is imperative *we grasp the vision God has for us.* We should get excited with what He wants to do in us and through us. We are who God said we are. We can do what God said we could do. We can have what God said we could have.

We are the only power that can stop it from coming to pass. What are our reasons for stopping it from coming to pass? Is it because we fear the devil so much? The biggest problem is that we don't understand God as much as we should. Is because we have never truly studied God to see what He said about Himself? If we did we would see what God said about Himself, our adversary and us. We would understand and we would have confidence in the call in our lives.

Many times we may wonder if Satan is omnipresent, all knowing, and all-powerful. Absolutely not! Then how is it that he is always in our lives? Well let's be honest, I am not that important that I draw the enemy's attention. The devil is not sitting in this throne room saying, "Oh my, there's that Henry Lewis again. Uh-oh, what am I going to do about this guy?"

No, he has bigger fish to fry. However, he does have somebody assigned to my life, to watch over everything I do and say. He does this to see if there is any potential of me causing him problems. He wants to see if I am believe God and His word or if I believe him (Satan) and his lies.

He wants to see if I have confidence in myself because I know who I am in Christ but more importantly I know who Christ is through me. Have I reached a point in my life where I realize I can do all things not because I am so spiritual but because Christ lives within me? As long as Christ lives in me, I can do all things through Christ who strengthens me and I can prosper.

When cancer came into my life the doctors, who had good intentions, told me that I would have to quit preaching because every time I use my voice, I steal the strength from my body. The only thing they wanted me to do was to stay home, rest, and watch television. Don't preach, don't work, don't walk, don't exercise, and don't drink a lot of water because you will end up drowning in your own fluids.

There were a lot of don'ts and they were not telling me what I could do. If I had listened to them, I would have gone home and died. Instead I listened to the word of God. I studied the word of God, and I asked the Lord how this came into me. How and why did this happen to me? Lord, you know I exercised all my life, and I never did drugs or smoked or drunk alcohol.

Lord, I respect my body, I didn't glorify my body, but I took good care of it. When I was a young man I followed a good diet. Why is this thing within me Father? No matter how much I depend on my body, no matter how good I follow my diet and avoid all harmful chemicals and alcohol, this cancer still found a way into me.

Why Lord? Then he reminded me that I was made up from the dust of the earth,(*Genesis 2:7*) and this body has weaknesses and is subjected to natural laws. Praise God my spirit is not subjected to natural laws like my body. My spirit is the real man, and this body is to be brought under subjection to my spirit and my spirit to the Holy Spirit and the word of God.

My body said I am tired, I am getting weak, I am not going to make it. My mind remains neutral because it never knows what to do. It follows the strongman; therefore, if my flesh is the strongest, it will follow the flesh. If the spirit is the strongest then it will submit to the spirit. When my body was proclaiming everything negative my mind was agreeing with it, but my spirit refused to listen to it.

My spirit said, "I can do all things through Christ who strengthens me. *(Philippians 4:13)* That before the foundation of the world the Lamb of God was slain, not only for my salvation, but also for my healing." *Isaiah* tells me that by His stripes I was made whole. In the New Testament it tells me that if I proclaim my health in the name of Jesus, whatsoever I ask the Father believing He shall give it to me. (***John 14:13***)

When the doctors were telling me how weak I was going to be, I was actually getting stronger, I stopped taking their medicines, but not because I had anything against them. Thankfully, God has given us doctors, but the medicine wasn't doing anything. It was stealing my strength. Hopefully it was killing the cancer but by attacking the cancer it was weakening my body.

I went through a lot of prayer about it. The first time I wanted to give it up. The Lord said no because if I gave it up then it would be out of frustration and not by faith. He told me to keep taking the medicine until I had the faith the give it up. Once we move into the realm of faith we will have no problems giving it up. A day came when I had filled myself with the word of God. I couldn't help but believe the Word of the Lord. I walked away by faith and it was six days later when I realized I hadn't taken the medicine.

Then I noticed my strength was returning to me. I was able to walk further. I was able to do things that for months I could not do. I never went back to the medicine; instead, I went back to the word of God. I began to believe I was who God said I was. I could do what God said I could, and I could have what God said I could have as long as I was walking in obedience to God.

I quit worrying what man said about me. I was only concerned with what God thought about me. I refused to believe what the enemy had to say about me. The adversary was working in my life through unbelief, through doubt, through fear. He was trying to make the cancer larger than it was. He was trying to make the heart problem larger and he kept trying to take away my hope and faith.

But the Lord told me that cancer had a name, and that heart condition had a name. And anything that has a name must bow to the name of Jesus and must obey it. Cancer had to give way and heart problems had to give way to the authority in the name of Jesus. Jesus said He came to give life and that more abundantly. The enemy knew what was going on in my life. Why, because he left you to afflict me? No, he had a spirit assigned to my life.

Wait: can't the enemy be in two places at one time?

While I was battling cancer, someone else was battling cancer too and someone else was going through a testing time.

The answer is quite simple; the enemy had one of his allies watching over this one and that one as he had once watching me.

 It was through his demonic spirit.

What you confess, you WILL possess

....

You will also declare a thing, and it **will** be established for **you**; So light **will** shine on ...

Step out in faith with me and **possess what you confess**. *Ezra 8:23*

What you fear the most, will come upon you

....

What I **fear most** overtakes me. What I dread happens to ... I am afraid of all my pains, I know that **You will** not acquit me. *Job 30:15*

 Worst of my **fears** has **come** true, what I've dreaded the **most**
Job 3:25

FEAR opens the gate for the enemy to afflict us

....

CHAPTER 17

.....The Ranks in Satan's Army.....

Now there are four different schools of thought on what demons are. But for this study we will hold on to the traditional teaching on what demons are. Demons, according to tradition and which has been taught in the churches for a long time, are fallen angels. One third of the angels fell with Lucifer and according to the church became demons. These angels fell from glory through the realms of heaven down to the earth where they became his army, his legions, and his eyes and ears.

Satan himself cannot be everywhere. Like a commander, he does not go to the front line. He stays back and sends his forces to work for him. In the military we don't put our general on the front line. We put him in the command tent where he issues his orders for his troops. If the general is taken out, then the power of the army is taken.

The American Indian understood this very well, which is why they kept their chiefs in the back. The cavalry also understood this and that is why they went after the chief. Once he was killed the Indians, now without leadership, would scatter.

The general is in the background with the other high-ranking officers making plans for the battle. These plans are then sent down through the chain of command like the captains, lieutenants, sergeants, then to the corporals and finally to the soldiers who are on the front lines. The front line soldier's responsibility is to carry out the orders of their superiors. The common soldier is to carry out the order no matter what the cost is to them. The officers, who may rank from the lieutenants to the generals, are protected. These officers are protected so they can continue making blueprints for victory.

Satan is like a general or commander, and he is in the second heaven where his throne is. This is where he rules and reigns. With him are the fallen angels who are his ruling officers. These principalities work with him to bring the battle to God and His people. The kingdom of Satan is completely organized. All of his orders are going through the ranks.

Ephesians 6:12 is where we find the ranking order of the kingdom of the adversary. They are the principalities, the wicked spirits, the power and the prince and power of the air. There are the fallen angels, who are referred to as strongmen, and they pass orders down to the earthbound demons, the spirit of infirmity, and the unclean spirit. These spirits are carrying out the orders and are fighting the battles on the front lines on the earth while the strongmen are fighting the battles in the heavenly places.

Does this make sense to you? This shows us how Satan is aware of us and how he inflicts us. It is not necessary that the devil himself come into our homes, and brings the battle directly to us. It is because he has his spirit of infirmity, his unclean spirit, and his familiar spirit, who roam the earth as in (*Matthew 12:43-45*).

In this passage of scripture it talks about the demons roaming the earth and looking for a place to rest or a house to inhabit. They torment mankind. They torment the unbeliever and they try to oppose the believer. They try to carry out the order of their master. They try to expand the kingdom of darkness for their master. They do whatever they can to hinder and to bind the saints of God by causing sickness, heartache, depression, and suicide, addiction to drugs and alcohol, and murder.

If you look at these different spirits they all have different names, and different attributes. We know according to (*Matthew 9:32-39*) that demons can infect sickness. In (*Mark 5)* we know that demons can inhabit animals. We know that animals are so repulsed by demons that even the pigs would prefer to take their lives rather than have the demons to live in them. Demons can possess and control human beings, hence the term demon possession.

Remember the young girl who was possessed by a fortune-telling spirit? In the King James Version it states this damsel was filled with the spirit of fortune telling, but in the Greek it states she was filled with the spirit of the python. We know that the python is considered to be a king of snakes and only the anaconda matches its size. This means it was no minor demon; instead, it was a rare occasion when a strongman took control of a person.

There are three times when a principality actually took control of a human. First was when Satan entered Judas Iscariot. Second was when a strongman took control of the young girl, and the third will be in the future when Satan enters the antichrist. On the average case of possession it is mainly the earthbound spirits called demons.

Now in the case of the young girl in the book of Acts, she came under the influence of a strongman and became his slave. There was no joy and no happiness in her young life until the day when one stronger than the strongman came on the scene. It was the name above every name, the name of Jesus, that set her free and brought the whole city into confusion and chaos.

Paul, just like Jesus, had power over the unclean spirits and over the whole kingdom of Satan because of the One who lived in Paul, the spirit of Jesus. Paul knew where his authority came from. It came from the Lord. Paul wrote this amazing statement – it is no longer I that lives but rather it is the spirit of Christ who lives it through me. How many of us have the confidence that it is no longer I that lives but Christ who lives this life through me?

Men like Ravenhill, Wigglesworth, Finney, Oswald Chambers, T.L. Osborne, David Wilkerson, Derek Prince, Dr. Roy Hicks, Grant Jeffrey, and Frank Hamlin understood this and they were able to do great things. Look at what Lester Sumrall did by faith. They did what they did because they understood they no longer lived but Christ lived in them. When you get this revelation too then you will also do great things for God's kingdom.

We must understand that demons can and will come into humans causing all kinds of problems. They can and will cause mental disorders, conflict, stress, and anxiety. They will even cause people to take their own lives. In Mark we see the man possessed by the spirit called Legion. The man was not in his right mind. As soon as Jesus rebuked the spirits they fled in fear into the pigs and the man was then in his right mind. This man went from being a maniac who had to be bound in chains for the safety of the people to being completely restored to his right mind. Not only was the inside of the man not clean but his outside was also clean as well.

Satan comes to steal, maim, rob, kill, and destroy man, who is created in God's image, but Jesus came to destroy the enemy's kingdom and to establish His Father's kingdom and restore man back to the Father. Demons, unlike many people and even some Christians, understand who Jesus is. They know that Jesus is the Holy One of God. They knew it when He defeated the adversary in the wilderness. They proclaimed it out loud when they said, "Jesus thou Son of the Most High."

James 2:9 tells us it is not enough to believe in God because even the devil believes though he can never be saved. You must not only believe in God you must also obey Him. There are two Hebrew words for listen. One means simply to hear and the other means to hear and then obey in all things. When we say we believe in God and we hear you Lord, we are not just taking it in our ears but into our hearts as well. We cannot just hear and do nothing about what we hear, we must act upon it and carry out the orders that are given. When we obey, it proves we heard and trust Him.

Demons can teach false doctrine. Where do you think all these religions come from? How do you think the devil keeps tabs on all the false religions? There are the Muslims, Buddhists, Hindus, Catholics, Jehovah Witnesses, Mormons, the Moonies, the Children of God, Scientologists, and so on. He is able to keep tabs on these false religions because he has his fallen angels to take charge of all these religions. His demons teach these religions to blind man and to keep fallen man in bondage.

Man will worship anything because he has a God-shaped vacuum in his heart. If he will not worship the God in heaven, then he will end up worshiping a cow. You will worship something. I don't care if you say you are an atheist. You will worship something. If you claim to be an atheist I can prove to you that you worship something. You may not worship God, but you probably worship money, power, or maybe a cow.

Even though you do not give a name to a god you worship, you still worship a god. He is called the god of this world and your god is a counterfeit and will lead you to damnation after your life of bondage. Even when an atheist comes among those who say they are unbelievers, they realize that he is still under someone's authority. He is following someone. He may say he doesn't believe, but as he begins to talk he shows he believes in something.

What the atheist believes is humanism and education. He puts his faith in his own wisdom and that is something he can never trust. If we want to trust wisdom, then trust the wisdom that comes from the Father of light – the only true and lasting wisdom there is. His wisdom will not fail us, but our wisdom will fail us.

Science and education is always changing. If we compare the books used to train young people today with the books we were taught by when we were in school, we will see that the principle of education is always changing. Even history books have been changed.

What doesn't change is the word of God. The word says heaven and earth will pass away but not one little dot of My word shall be changed. God's word never changes and God's wisdom never changes or fades. If we want to have a solid foundation to put our faith in, put it in God's word because it will never fail you.

Understand This

....

Demons are real and whatever we consider a demon to be. It doesn't matter what we believe Satan to be, whether we think he is a fallen angel or a god. He is very real and he is our enemy. He is operating in our life to destroy our families and us. He is out to keep us inflicted and to kill our children.

Are you a watchmen? Being a guardsmen?

Be alert and of sober mind. Your enemy the devil prowls around like a roaring lion looking for someone to devour. (*I Peter 5:8*)

CHAPTER 18

.....Everything Wrong In The World – An Act of God?.....

It is always amazes me that when the people of the world hear about something terrible like a wild fire, or a massacre, or a terrible storm, or a death of a child, they always refer to it as an act of God. People who have lost a child constantly ask – why did God take my child? I have personally lost four children and a granddaughter but it was not God who took them.

People become angry with a child molester, a serial killer, and a drug pusher. They want them to be caught and punished. Yet when the greatest enemy of our family makes his way into them, we don't get excited at all. We don't get angry and demand his arrest, or his punishment. Instead we deny his existence.

We allow him to continue to bring chaos into our lives. We let him divide the husband against the wife and the children against the parents. He is turning our children into drug addicts, thieves and robbers, drug pushers, murderers, and members of the many different cults and occult religion. He wants to enslave our daughters by taking them from the precious purpose they were created for and put them on open display.

I will not get vulgar by describing what he does with our daughters and also with many of our sons. He causes our children to be unsure of their gender and they live a counterfeit lifestyle such as boys believing they are girls trapped in a masculine body or girls thinking they are men trapped in a woman's body. They believe the lie sold to them by the enemy. We don't become upset over this. We don't make war on the adversary and demand he be arrested and punished. We say he doesn't exist yet the evidence of his existence is everywhere.

What God's word proclaims him to be is proven in the lives of our families. We should be angrier with him than at the human criminals because all they can steal is our physical stuff. Satan steals not only the physical and emotional but he also steals the spiritual as well. When are we going to wake up and realize we have been enslaved and tricked by a being that doesn't care about our family or us at all? When will we come to the realization that we have a real invisible enemy that despises us?

Mankind will embrace any religious philosophy but the truth. Let a man or woman of God stand in your presence and proclaim God's word. Instead of receiving it with joy and thanksgiving, we will laugh and ridicule them. Instead of being angry with the enemy who comes to enslave, steal from, and even kill our family, we become angry and bitter towards the representatives of the kingdom of God. We demand that their mouths be silent while we continue to listen to the voice of our cruel master.

I am speaking mainly to the people who don't believe. We become offended at the Ten Commandments and demand they be taken down. We become offended at God's word so we demand it not be taught in public places. We become angry with the God who created us, and we demand that He should not be worshipped or praised.

Yet the god who steals our children and our peace and joy and turns our lives into a living hell, we tolerate. We allow his religion to be spread like cancer throughout the entire world. We don't ask for his laws to be taken down or for the heathen's books that spread spiritual poison to be destroyed. We accept them. We don't demand that the occult books be destroyed and we don't declare that the Buddhist or Hindu religion needs to be done away with. We don't ask for the followers of the false cults to be stopped and not allow them to teach their lies.

Why is it we are only offended by the God of Christianity? Why is it when something happens negative in our lives the only God whose name we use as a curse is the name of Jesus? Why is it that the only God that offends us is the God of the Hebrew and Christian? Why doesn't the name of any other god offend us? It really is very simple. The false god of this world has blinded us. Our perceptions and our understanding have become perverted and we see our enemy as our friend.

My Bible tells me that while I was a far off God loved me and sent His Son to die for me. No other god in any other religion has done that. Well, Brother Lewis, how do you know that? I have spent a lifetime in studying religion, even before I became a Christian. I studied and mastered the different religions and their philosophies and concepts. I knew their gods but none of their gods or goddesses so loved me while I was a far off. Even while I was an enemy they didn't love me enough to send their son to die for me.

Only the God of Christianity did that for me and He did that to destroy the works of the devil. (The one who does what is sinful is of the devil, because the devil has been sinning from the beginning. The reason the Son of God appeared was to destroy the devil's work) *I John 3:3*

He did it to give us life and that more abundantly. He came to bring joy and happiness into our lives. Every time God delivers us from something He replaces it with something better. If we could grab a hold of the love, compassion, mercy and the unending grace the God of Creation has for us, we would run to His arms. We would flee from the god of oppression as quickly as we could.

We would bring nothing with us. We would leave it all behind as the Apostle Paul did and count it as nothing. We would run to Him and never want to leave His presence because we would come to understand that His love for us is unconditional. He has only good intentions for us. He would never leave us or harm us. He would only bless us. He doesn't send His anointing spirit to trouble us, or afflict us, or put diseases on us.

Please understand that God has put this message in me. It has nothing to do with my personal opinion. Take time and do a comparison of God with any god of this world. He has sent his allies to spy on us and to destroy our families and us. He imposes his will upon us, puts sickness on us, robs from us, and kills us.

He sent his messengers to spy on us and to keep us in despair and hopelessness. He accuses us and keeps our weaknesses in front of us to keep us in bondage.

Every time we try to think a positive thought about ourselves the enemy will whisper a negative factor in our ears. He does everything he can do to keep us in bondage and we serve him faithfully. Yet the God of Creation sent His Son to die for us on the cross so we don't have to pay the price for our rebellion. He allowed Him to be beaten and to be put to open shame.

He does all this so we can be redeemed. After Jesus is dead and buried, He rises from the grave to ascend on high, and when He gets back to His heavenly home with His Father, He sends His Spirit to teach us and empower us. He sends gifts from on high to help us. He sends His ministering spirits, His angels, to help us. They are not sent to spy on us to hurt us or to tattle tell on us. They are sent to strengthen us, encourage us, and to help us stand. They run to the battle on our behalf and we despise God. Is there not something wrong here? Should we not love God and despise our old slave master?

Can we not see His grace and love toward us*? But God commendeth **his love toward us***, in that, while we were yet sinners, Christ ... And if, by Divine **grace***, they were thus brought to repent, and to believe in **Romans 5:8**

Can we not embrace Him and love Him for what He has done for us? I pray for those who do not know Him. I pray their eyes are open to truth, and they see the love of God and the false ways of Satan and his deception he's had for mankind from Adam to the last man born.

CHAPTER 19

.....Submit to God, Resist The Devil and He Will Flee From You..... James 4:7

For those of us who are born again, I pray that we move on to spiritual maturity leaving behind the old ways of the flesh and moving on to the way of the Spirit.(*Philippians 3:13*) I pray we come to understand the great blessing He has given to us so we'll know who we are because of the one who lives in us. I pray we never confess we are lower than the belly of a worm and that we realize we are all sons and daughters of the living God.

For those who do not know my God, my great Savior the Lord Jesus Christ, I pray that confusion, spiritual blindness, and spiritual deafness be bound in your life. I loose you to spiritual clarity of sight so you can see the one who is trying to control you and separate you from God and what he is, and for you to be able to hear what the spirit of God is saying.

I pray for the unbeliever to get a revelation of who the enemy is and what he is doing to your family and that you get a revelation of my God and what He wants to do in your life. Once you see this you will understand and run to God and embrace Him.

I have tried to give insight into the plan of the enemy by showing where his throne is, how he works in the life of the believer and the unbeliever. We've seen how Satan has been able to deceive so many people and how his organization of demons works. I've tried to show you where Satan came from and how he become what he is today. He is powerful and outside of the triune God we would not stand a chance against him. There is nothing on **this earth** that can stand against him. It is only through the **name of Jesus** and by **the power of the Holy Spirit** we can overcome him.

Only those of us who are born again and Spirit-filled can stand against him. We understand that the enemy is relentless and determined to establish his kingdom and fulfill his goal to destroy us. Satan has **almost** unlimited power at his disposal. He is **not** omniscient, omnipotent, or omnipresent.

He does have a well-organized army under his control and as we look at him we can clearly see that without God we are hopeless against him. So how do we deal with or what can we do against so powerful of an enemy if he is as powerful as he has been portrayed through the word of God and the opinion of man. In James 4:7 it tells us to submit ourselves therefore to God. In other words, we are to bring our lives under order and obedience to God. We are to humble ourselves under God and draw near to Him, resist the devil and he shall flee from us.

Refuse to give in to the enemy. Refuse to listen to him. Refuse to follow after him. Refuse to have anything to do with him or his kingdom. Yes! Resist the devil and he will flee from you. We have the ability to do this. God tells us in His word that if we stand up against the adversary and resist him in the name of Jesus he has to flee from us.

Resisting is when we refuse to do what the devil wants and we stand against him with all of our ability and strength and refusing to give any ground to him no matter what. Refuse to submit to his influence over our lives. It doesn't mean he will not come against us. It simply means we have taken a strong stance against him and his army. They will no longer control us. They will not bring us back under their authority ever again. To resist the devil is to stand and refuse to listen to him.

The first way we can resist him is to close our eye gates to the filth he tries to ensnare us with. The next is to close our ears to his voice and do not obey him or let him lead us astray. Don't let him misguide you. Do not let him put ideas into your head. If we feel the urge to go and pray do not let him stop you.

Do not allow him to bring confusion into your life. Stop your ears against his foolishness. Refuse to listen to his slanderous remarks, his false accusations, and his lies. Stand against him with the word of God. When he tells you what you cannot do, show him what you can do through God's word. I can do all things through Christ who strengthens me.

Do not use your own opinion or your favorite philosophy because you will never win an argument against Satan using these. He will easily take them apart. When he tells you that you are nothing and that you are lower that the belly of a worm, tell him – I am more than a conqueror through Christ Jesus and no weapon formed against me shall proper.

I am more than an over comer I am a child of God. I have been redeemed from the curse of the law. I have been redeemed from death, hell, and the grave. I have been redeemed from poverty. I have victory in my life though Jesus Christ my Lord and Savior. I sit in heavenly places ruling and reigning with Him. I have the authority of the kingdom of heaven backing me. I have the right to use the name of Jesus. I have the power of attorney to use Jesus' name in prayer to guarantee the victory in everything.

I am not the tail. I am the head
....

I am not defeated. I am not overcome. I am not a weakling. I am not the tail. I am the head. *(Deuteronomy 28:13)* I am not beneath. I am above. I am more than a conqueror through Christ who strengthens me. The victory is mine for it has already been won for me. It was not won through my knowledge or understanding and not through my own strength. It has been won through Jesus Christ, my Lord, for me. He has won all the battles. He has conquered death, hell, and the grave. The keys of the kingdom of darkness have been taken from you, Satan. You rule nothing in my life anymore. Your power over me is broken. You have no authority because I am no longer your slave. I am now a child of God.

Stand and resist the adversary of your life and the destroyer of your family. How do you resist him and stop him? You refuse to listen to Him and to obey him. Refuse to be brought under subjection to him. Anything you allow to dominate you is your master.

If you are addicted to alcohol, it is your master. If you surrender yourselves to sex and drugs, they have become your master. You may think you are in control over these things like nicotine for example, but you are blind to the truth. Instead you are the slave and they are your masters.

Refuse to allow Satan to have that power over you. If you are addicted to anything remember they are tools used by the enemy to control you. Stand up against them. Keep in mind! At one time you made the choice to start this bad habit, you can make the decision to stop. These inanimate objects do not have the power in themselves to sway you in any way. It is the adversary using these things to hold you in bondage. Refuse to obey him any longer. Walk away from it.

In *Ephesians 6:13* we are told we can stand against him, that when the enemy comes we don't have to run from him. We do not have to bow or surrender to him. We can stand and stand strong with our loins girded with the gospel of truth. We can in the strength of God Almighty. We can stand in the power of His word. We can stand in the strength of His Holy Spirit.

We can have peace of mind because we have the mind of Christ in us. You will keep in perfect peace those whose minds are steadfast, because they trust in you. *(Isaiah 26:3)*. We can resist him. We can stand against him. We can push him back and stop him from advancing. We can be sure that through the word of God and the name of Jesus that he will not make any more advancement.

    (**I Corinthians 2;16**) I can choose my thoughts and think things on purpose

    It is not possible for you to establish a boundary; in other words, a line which Satan cannot cross. Let God put a hedge around you that will stop him in his tracks. If you are hidden in God, and God is in you and the word abides in you, then you can stand against the devil. The spirit of Christ is within you to strengthen you to live a victorious life, and the Holy Spirit is in you to teach you the things of God; therefore, you can live in victory.

    Remember what scripture says – the Lord is your strength and your salvation.(***Psalms 28:7***) God is your shield and His word is your sword. He is your refuge and strong tower, your place of rest and healing. The Lord is the banner over you. He is your deliverer and your provider. God is your – everything. He is your Sabbath.

    The Sabbath is a time of rest.(***Hebrews 4:9***) How do we enter our rest? We enter the Sabbath and hide ourselves in God. We place ourselves into God. When the enemy tries to draw you out and to get you to stop hiding in the Lord, stand strong and refuse. The Lord is your city of refuge.

    In the Old Testament if a man committed a crime by accident and if he could get to one of the ten cities set up as cities of refuge, he could abide in that city and the avengers of blood could not harm him as long as he was in that city. Those who were assigned or took it upon themselves to bring this man back into bondage and then kill him were now powerless against him, as long as he remained in that city of refuge.

God is our city of refuge, our hiding place. (*Numbers 35, Joshua 20, Deuteronomy 4, 19*) When the devil comes against you, don't try to stand against him in your own strength or in your own knowledge. Run to the Lord, hide in Him, and let Him fight for you. If you stay under the shed blood of Jesus the enemy cannot touch you.

Satan can yell, scream, and call you every name in the book. He can bring all the accusations he wants. He can accuse as much as he can to the Father. It will do him no good, for as long as you are under the blood you are hidden from him. There is a hedge of protection around you that he cannot penetrate. He cannot pass through it.

Do not break the hedge!

In the book of **Job** it said, "He that breaks a hedge shall be bitten by a serpent." The only one who can break a hedge is yourself, and if you do break the hedge because of your own foolishness, then you expose yourself to the enemy.(*Ecclesiastes 10:8*) Do not break the hedge.! Do not allow him to trick you into doing so. Stay hidden in the Lord. Let the Lord cover you. Stay sheltered in Him. The enemy will try to provoke you. He will ask you what are you doing and then mock you by saying that all you are doing is hiding behind Jesus.

What better place is there than to hide in Christ? Stay there. He is the one who has already defeated the enemy. Christ is the one who has already established all victories. In Christ is our place of strength. It is there that you operate, not in your feeble power, but in the awesome strength of Jesus.

Stepping away from Jesus is like the man who left the city of Jerusalem and began to descend down to Jericho. Do you remember the parable of the man who left Jerusalem, the city of God, and began to make his way to Jericho, the city cursed by the Lord? On his way down to Jericho thieves fall upon him, take everything from him and leave him naked and bruised, near death.

We know how the scribe and the priest just passed him by; however, a Good Samaritan, who by social prejudices should have avoided him, stopped and took care of his wounds, and placed him on his own donkey. He took the injured man to an inn paid for the cost of the room and promised the inn keeper that he pay him on his way back if any extra cost may have accrued.

This man who was beaten and left for dead had departed from the city of God where no one could beat and rob him. He chose to leave the protection of God where he was protected from things like thieves and robbers. No one could touch him as long as he was within the city's walls, the protection of God. He chose to leave the city of God and to head down to a city strongly cursed by God.

This was a place where only vile creatures, unclean spirits, jackals, owls, and haunts dwelled. It was a habitation of every type of demon. Why was he leaving the presence of God and going there to begin with? Since he made the choice to get out from the protection of God, he exposed himself to thieves, robbers, and murderers and placed his life in jeopardy.

Thank God the Lord arranged for a Good Samaritan (*Luke 10:5-37*) to come along at the right time. The Samaritan was coming from the city of Jericho to the city of God. He was leaving the corrupt city and going to the city of God. The man he met was doing the opposite of what he was doing. The man leaving God's presence should have known better than going into the presence of the adversary and his allies. He put himself in jeopardy and danger, but God had mercy on him.

He was not only being brought back to the Lord but he was placed in the merciful hands of a man who would care for him and see to it that every need he had was provided for. Sometimes we do foolish things like leaving the covering of God. The devil doesn't have the ability to touch us as long as we are under the covering of God. Sometimes we leave it not knowing why we allow ourselves to be deceived by the enemy and lose out from the protection of the Lord.

When you leave God's shelter, you begin to descend downward, leaving everything of God behind. There is nowhere to go but down. When you are in the presence of God, you go continually up from the mountaintop to mountaintop, from high place to high place.

Sadly when you allow yourself to be led and deceived by the enemy, he will quickly jump on you and try to destroy you. He will do the same thing to you as he did to man in the parable who left God's protection.

In *Genesis 4:7* God warns Cain that sin lies waiting for the opportunity to leap on him and destroy him. Do not let the enemy deceive you. The best defense is an offense. Instead of waiting for the enemy to put his army in order so he can put his plans together to come against you, bring the battle to him. According to *Acts 10:38 and John 3:8*, get on the offensive. Do not wait for the enemy to make the first move. Don't let the enemy have his way. The gates of hell shall not prevail against the church of God.

Remember, gates do not move, they do not advance toward us. We advance toward them. Go out and do what God told you to do. Brother Lewis, you just told us not to allow ourselves to be brought from out of the protection of God. That is absolutely correct but you can go forward bringing the gospel of Jesus everywhere God sends you without leaving the covering of God. You can hide in the Lord. You can abide in the shadow of the Almighty. You can rest in God even as you labor for the Lord, by going forth to bring those in bondage to freedom. Go forth in the Lord and in the strength of His Spirit, just make sure He is going with you.

Do not leave Him behind and go on your own. As you start to go forward and start to bring the battle to the enemy, do it with God before you. Let Him be your shield and buckler. Let Him fight for you and through you because then you are guaranteed a victory. For the LORD your God is the one who goes with you to fight for you against your enemies to give you victory.(*Deuteronomy 20:14*.) God wants to be your strong town, your healer, and your protector. He wants to cover you, to direct you, and to guide you. Let Him tell you everything you need to know on every step of the way.

Do not run ahead of Him. Do not leave Him behind whatsoever you do.

Make sure He is alive in you, behind you, in front of you and under you. Go forward, and go in confidence, but go with God. Make sure you have not moved out of His protection.

Make sure you have not allowed your own flesh to blind you to the fact you have left Him behind and your moving on your own in your own strength because if you have then you will be defeated.

If your moving with the Lord, then wherever you go shall become the Lord's. You will be able to take back everything the Lord has given you and the enemy has stolen.

Declare war on whatever has been keeping you from recovering what you should never forfeit to the darkness.

Maybe you've been accepting a loss that you never should have surrendered to. You know what God is saying? It's time to fight back, and realize that the Messiah, Jesus, who descended from David, has the power to "bring everything back." You're no match for this enemy from hell, but he's no match for your Jesus!

And Jesus told us that we could pray and bind that strong man, and one stronger than he is (speaking of Jesus himself) will come and overpower him and take away his possessions. Those are possessions he never should have had in the first place. The enemy may have his hand on something or someone right now he has no right to.

It's time for you to follow General Jesus into the battle to take back what the enemy has stole

CHAPTER 20

.....Obey the Lord and Stand Firm.....
I Corinthians 15:58, 2 Chronicles 20:20

In the Old Testament when David was out with the Philistines to fight against Saul, the armies of the opposing kings came and took Ziklag and all of the women and children.(*I Samuel 27*) When David got back and saw the destruction of Ziklag and the women and children were taken captive. But the Lord told him to go and that he will take back everything that was taken with no loss of anything.

David, because he was obedient to God and did it the way God told him to, was able to recover everything the enemy had taken. A valuable lesson we learn from this is that while David was protecting his front, he left his rear exposed and the enemy came in. It is so important to be sure the Lord has us completely covered. David was able to recover everything because he stood with the Lord and followed the Lord and was victorious.

The same thing could happen to you. The enemy may be able to find a way and break in because that is what a thief does. He will not come in the way you expect him too. He doesn't ask your permission. He breaks in and takes what he can, and then he runs away. Once you become aware of him and what has happened and you confront the thief he has to return what he stole. Not only does he return what he stole but according to God's word and law, he must return greater than what he stole from you.

The scriptures state when the thief is found out he must return twice of what he stole.

In some cases in scripture he must give back seven times more that what he has stolen. When you confront the enemy in the authority of the Lord, he must return not only what he stole from you, but he also has to give interest on it. Ask the Lord what you should do how you should fight this battle, then listen and let God direct you.

Please understand the enemy is not invincible, he can be defeated and overcome. ***Revelation 12:11*** says they over came him (Satan) by the word of their testimonies and the blood of the Lamb. You are victorious when you proclaim what God has done in your life or when you stand up and bear witness to the goodness, grace, mercies, and kindness of your God. Tell people about the love of God and how He brought them from the dungeon, the miry clay, or from the garbage pit and set their feet on the rock.

Jesus Christ is the solid rock of our faith. God took us from being slaves and cleaned us up. He made us a royal nation, priests and kings in His kingdom. We are vessels of honor unto Him. Our testimonies drive back the enemy and make him crazy. He cannot stand it when the children of God stand up and give forth the victory in their life and of the great things God has done.

The Old Testament tells us over and over again to remember the goodness of God and the wonderful things

He has done. If we remember what the Lord had done for us yesterday then we will have confidence that He will do it for us today and tomorrow. If God has delivered us from the oppression of the enemy, He will do it for us again and again. When we allow God him, or ask him to, or place our hand into His hand, He will deliver us. We cannot be over come by anything.

You may go through the fire and through the flood but they will not destroy you or consume you because God goes with you. Once you understand that God is walking with you, and then you can see how you are moving from victory to victory with His help. Your joy will be present when you remind the enemy what God did for you and then you apply the blood of the Lamb.

The enemy cannot touch you.(*I John 5:18*) You have been redeemed. When the enemy accuses you of something you are not guilty, or tries to remind you of who you used to be, then you remind him that you have been redeemed by the sacrifice of the Lamb, washed in the blood, and filled with His Spirit.

You are not that person of yesterday. You are a new creature in Christ Jesus.(*II Corinthians 5:17*) You serve a new God. You have a new Father, and the enemy has nothing within you. His power and authority has been broken over your life once and for all. The only chance that he has to influence your life or to bring chaos, confusion, or destruction is if you give him the rights to do it. The only weapon that he can use against the child of God is the weapon we give to him to use against us.

All other weapons must fall harmlessly to the ground according to God's word. They will not prevail against the body of Christ. If Satan attacks us one way, he will flee from us in seven different ways. We are shielded and protected by the blood of Jesus. Satan cannot get through the power of the blood. We also have the name of Jesus to use against him and he cannot stand against it. At the mention of His name every knee must bow and every tongue confess that Jesus is Lord to the glory of God the Father.

Therefore, if you hang around much longer, Satan, we will just have to preach a sermon to you. Listen to the great things God has done in our lives or flee; the choice is yours. Chances are he will flee from you. All power and authority has been given to you by Jesus Himself according to *Matthew 28:18; 16:19 and 2 Timothy 1:7.* God has given you the power of the blood covenant forever and forever. It is yours. If you understand this then you must realize there is no power on earth, no power in the oceans, no power in the heavens, or no power in hell itself can overcome you or stop you.

You have the guarantee of God's word you will go through everything. It doesn't mean you won't have trials and tribulations. God simply said you would be victorious because God goes through it with you. Remember what God has delivered you from and remember the good thing God has done for you. If you look back over your life, by God's grace you can see the difference between who you were a year ago and who you are today.

Accept what God has given you such as the authority, the power, the anointing, and the Holy Spirit to teach you all things. It is the Spirit of Christ in you that strengthens you to live the Christ life.(***Romans 8:11***) You also have the mind of Christ so you can make the right decisions.(***I Corinthians 2:16***) He is strength, wisdom, and knowledge. The revelation, the illumination, and the inspiration all come from Him. The word of wisdom, word of knowledge, prophecy, tongues, and interpretation of tongues, healings and workings of miracles were given to us for the edification and up lifting of the body of Christ. (***I Corinthians 12:8***)

He has not left you alone. (***Deuteronomy 31:6***) The presence of the Spirit and His word abide with you.

Stand and be an over comer.(***1 John 4:4***) God has not given you a weak mind but a strong spirit and a sound mind. He does this so nothing can prevail against you (***2 Timothy 1:7***). Don't fight from weakness because you are not the old man or the slave anymore. You fight from a position of power. You are a son or a daughter. You are royalty. The enemy has nothing over you that you don't allow him to.

I can't stress this point strong enough – You are no longer the first Adam <u>because</u> you are of the second Adam

••

The only victory the enemy can have over you is what YOU give to him. When you finally make up your mind that you are not going to be defeated anymore, then you will have the victory you have been promised by God. You will be more than an over comer. The enemy can be defeated. Please keep in mind God has given you more than you will ever need.

Jesus was ministering to the people and doing great things like healing the sick and opening the eyes of the blind. He also set a man free from demon possession. After teaching the people Jesus decides to get in the boat and cross over to the other side. Once he is in the boat, he falls asleep.

From out of nowhere a storm comes up. The disciples are scared. Jesus is sleeping soundly because he has had a busy day. The disciples are scared so they wake Jesus up. They become filled with fear and negative thoughts. Immediately they begin to pronounce destruction and how they are not going to make it to the other side. They exclaim, "Lord, don't you care that we perish."

In their fear, the disciples are telling Jesus they were going to perish and began to accuse Jesus of not caring. Was the Lord concerned or worried or scared? No! Did the enemy and his plans of destruction catch him off guard? No, He simply got up and spoke to the wind and the winds immediately ceased and the waters calmed and they were on the other side of the lake.

Have you ever wondered why Jesus could rest in the midst of the great storm? To better understand let's look at the word used to describe the storm. It is only used two times in the whole Bible, once in the Old Testament and once in the New Testament. The word used for storm here describes what it really was.

It was a malevolent spirit of destruction sent to kill Jesus before His time. This was not a natural physical storm. It was an extremely powerful principality out to stop the Lord's ministry. It was not none other than the prince and power of the air, the adversary himself. It was the enemy's full intention to destroy that little boat and Jesus never got rattled. He only paid attention to it when the disciples in fear woke him up.

He didn't even have a conversation. He simply brought everything to a stand still with three words: Peace, be still! Just that fast the storm was over and the enemy was defeated. Jesus never got concerned or rattled no matter what was going on. The reason Jesus could be this way was the awesome relationship He had with the Father. Before Jesus did anything, He always separated Himself so He could have communion with God the Father.

Jesus told the people that the words they heard Him speak were not His. They are what He hears His Father say. These deeds they see Him do are what He sees His Father do. Jesus set aside His own will and imitated the Father in everything the Father said and did. He never spoke His own words or His own opinion. He spoke what He heard His Father say.

Jesus knew if His Father gave Him a commandment or an order, He would give Jesus the power and authority to carry it out. Jesus had an order from the Father and that is why he knew what was waiting for Him on the other side.

Jesus knew as soon as he touched down he would be met by the demoniac and Satan's power over that man would be broken forever.(*Mark 5:1-20*) He knew He would set the man free and break the adversary's power because the Father commissioned him. He knows that since He was ordered by His Father to get there then the Father would make sure He got there.

Now I have written all this so that I could bring this back to you. You have received the commission to go forth to destroy the kingdom of Satan and to establish the kingdom of God and to bring men to God. God has given you an order to go. (*Colossians 1:25, Matthew 28-16-20*) Nothing can stop you. God will not because He told you to go. The devil cannot because you have been given authority over everything that exalts itself against God. The only one who can stop you is you. Remember, it was not you who gave the order to lay hands on the sick, to open the eyes of the blind, to cause the lame to walk, and to raise the dead.

It was God who gave the commission to you. As He did for Jesus He will do for you. Don't try doing it in your own way. Do it like Jesus did. Get away to be with the Father watch Him. Listen to how He speaks and then copy Him in all that He says and does. I hear your question – we are on the earth and God is in heaven. How will we be able to see him and hear him? My answer is: the same way Jesus did. Draw away for a time to be with your Father through prayer, praise, and worship. This brings us into the court of God, right into the Holy of Holies.

We are seated far above all principalities that everything is beneath our feet. "And the God of peace shall

bruise **Satan under your feet** shortly. The grace of our
Lord Jesus Christ be with you " (***Romans 16:20***)
We are sitting with Jesus ruling and reigning now, not
tomorrow, now. (***Matthew 28:16-20***) You may reject this
and say it was just a parable and keep living in defeat, or
you can accept the word of God as truth and live the
overcoming life. We need to get this into our spirit that God
has given us a commission and the power to carry out the
mission. The only thing stopping us is our own doubts,
fears and feelings of unworthiness. God is not a man that
He should lie or the Son of man that He should change His
mind. His yeas are yea and His nays are nay.

Jesus was the only true Son of God and the enemy
tries to stop him with a storm from doing what His Father
wanted Him to do. If Satan dares to attack the only
begotten Son of God how much more will he attack us, the
adoptive children? He sees our weaknesses, our doubts, our
fears, our insecurities and our luke warmness. He sees our
double mind.

How can we be on the earth and in heaven at the
same time?

How can I be walking with men under the assault of
the enemy and his principalities?

What is the storm the enemy is using on you? Is it
double-mindedness, is it fear of being ridiculed or is it a
fear of failure? This is only a storm! Is it cancer or some
other illness?

Remember, you may have cancer or some other afflicting disease, but it doesn't have you!

The real you is inside of you joined with the Holy Spirit..

No weapon shall prosper against you. **Isaiah 54:17**

CHAPTER 21

.....Whose Report Will You Believe?.....

I want to close this book with a question for you and me. **Whose report shall we believe?** The adversary who is a liar, a thief, and a murderer from the beginning says you are earthbound and powerless and will never amount to anything. All of these promises are for others like your pastor and the elders; it's not for you. If you try you will only get hurt worse than if you fail and you will be the laughing stock of the church. What will your family think? They have been going there for years and none of that crazy fanatical stuff ever happens.

As I said before if anyone should know this it would be the pastor and the elders and none of them are doing it and neither are they interested in it either. No, just set still like a good boy or girl and stop all this foolishness. Don't you know all of this passed away with the original disciples? Or will you believe the report of the Lord that says I can do all things through Jesus who strengthens me, because the Spirit of Christ lives in me to give me the strength to live the overcoming life, and the Holy Spirit fills me to overflowing to teach all the ways of the kingdom of God.

All I have to do is obey and God does the rest. God said that I am responsible to obey His orders and He, not I, is responsible for the miracle. I choose to be mocked by man, but accepted by God. I refuse to listen to the lies of Satan telling me I cannot do what God said I could do or that I cannot be what God said I am. I am more than a conqueror through Christ.

Men may laugh at me in my presence, call me names, ridicule me, and even strike me because they don't want to hear the truth. You can laugh in my face, but be warned if you refuse to believe God and let the devil keep you in bondage to a lie, there is a day coming soon when Satan and all whom he has deceived will cry in the face of God, the one whose friendship and power you have rejected for the lie of the enemy. May God give us all the courage to believe His word and the wisdom to reject the lies of Satan.

Someone may say that Satan was strong enough to crucify Christ. Let me tell you the crucifixion of Christ was not the devil's plan because if he would have understood what was going to happen when Christ would be crucified he would never have done it. Well what about all those Christians who were so faithful and yet they all died, why didn't they have power over death? It is appointed for man to die and then the judgment. These people were faithful and did not love their lives more than God.

I personally know thousands who wouldn't deny Christ in the face of torture because they were crucified, shot, beheaded and locked in their church and burned to death. If you could call them back they would all tell you they would do it again and again so the name of Christ would be exalted and His Father's kingdom be expanded. Where is your treasure stored here on earth where rust can destroy it or thieves can rob it or in heaven where no one can touch it? Where your treasure is there is where your heart will be also.

Do you remember the reason why Satan hates you so much? Do you recall what happened before the creation of earth and man? God had created three archangels. The first is Michael, the warrior of God and the defender of Israel. The second angel is Gabriel, the messenger of God. He was God's personal messenger sent to **_Daniel_** in the Old Testament and to many in the B'rit Hadashah (New Testament) including **Zechariah,** the husband of Elizabeth.

The _third angel is called Heyel_ (**Strong 1966, 1984**). The name _means container of the glory of God_ or the reflection of God. He was given the right to speak on the behalf of God and when he opened his mouth to speak all of heaven listened to him because of the glory that was in him. He was created the wisest, the most beautiful, and the strongest of all Bene Elohim the sons of God.

He had the honor of guarding the throne of God and guaranteeing that no one got an audience with the King of the universe unless invited to do so. He was also responsible to lead worship. He was an actual living organ so that when he moved his wings music played. He was the reward of eternal fellowship with the Godhead but it was not enough for him he wanted to be greater than his Creator.

Pride filled his heart and Michael, God's warrior, cast him down.

We know Michael is still God's warrior; the defender of Israel and Gabriel is still the messenger of God. These two have remained faithful, but the third angel who had the greatest blessing has fallen to pride and every gift he had has been given to **you**.

You now have everything he once had but has no more. You are the container of God's glory and the worshipper of God. You have the honor to come before God anytime you wish and you can bring others before the throne as well. Everything Satan once had you now have. You are on the way to heaven where Satan as Heyel once was. You have been delivered from hell and the lake of fire, which is the final destiny of Satan and those who follow him.

Satan hates you so much because everything he once had, you now have. When he sees you he remembers all he had and lost and never will have again. Remember, the very triune God, Creator of all things lives in you. He has given you great power and authority to go out and do something for your Father's kingdom.

May God open your eyes to truth and deliver you from bondage and make you a mighty warrior who is prepared to run to the battle when you are called.

God Bless

Dedicated Song

Lyrics from ***Run To The Battle***
Written by: Steven John Camp
Copyright: Word Music LLC

Chorus
Some people want to live
Within the sound of chapel bells
But I want to run a mission
A yard from the gates of hell

And with everyone you meet
I'll take the gospel and share it well
And look around you as you hesitate
For another soul just fell, let's run to the battle
Run to the battle

Verses
Do you have your armor on?
We're in the middle of a raging war
We've been training for so long
Have we learned to use His word?

We may not be ready but we serve a mighty Lord
And He's made us more than conquerors
So what are you waiting for? Let's run to the battle
We got to run, run to the battle

He has trampled down the enemy
And has given us the victory
When we pray we learn to see that His army

We are marching on our knees

There'll be times when we grow weak
Let's keep our faith alive
Let your faces shine with glory
For He's helped us to survive

And in that final hour when you feel like you're ready to
die
Will you hear the trumpet sound
Will you hear the warrior cry, run to the battle
We got to run, run to the battle

Chorus

About the Author

Dr. Henry Lewis is the President of an Apostolic International ministry called Joshua International. Joshua International offers Biblical Leadership Training and Spiritual Over comers material. Henry Lewis is a Sicilian Jew and a descendent of Andrew Murray.

He is married to his wife, Patricia, for over 42 years. They have been in ministry since 1980 and have two children.

Dr. Lewis has authored 10 books. The first book called A Quest for Spiritual Power is now translated in Arabic and in French. The Arabic book was printed in Egypt and the French book was assembled and translated in Switzerland and printed in France.

Dr. Lewis is a sought-after speaker and author, teaching at churches and conferences along with numerous TV guest media outlets teaching on subjects such as: spiritual warfare, revival, transformation, revelation, transformational prayer. Henry evangelizes and teaches with international prophetic leaders in 10 countries.

His testimony of his former occult leadership experiences of seven generations has enabled him to share the love of God and his delivering power.

Charisma magazine shared is testimony in 2000. 750,000 Hindus translated the article in their language and accepted Christ.

Dr. Lewis attended several colleges which led to obtain three Doctorates in Counseling, Theology and Christian Education.

Henry and his wife have established churches in the US. Their first church was by the assistance of Aimee Semple McPherson's son, Rolf McPherson, who believed in their calling. Later, Dr. Roy Hicks, Sr.

(friend who worked at Angelius Temple with Rolf
McPhearson) supported them as well.

Henry and Patricia's spiritual foundation was formed from: Dr. Leonard
Heroo (Apostle and President of Zion Bible Institute), McPherson),
Evangelist Robert Schambach, Prophet David Wilkerson and Derek
Prince, Lester Sumrall etc.

Henry's passionate thirst for the knowledge and truth of God's word led
him to obtain a deep relational experience with his Lord and Savior,
Jesus Christ – and not a religion – so he could hear and know the voice
of God.

His vision is to teach and train a courageous generation the
incorruptible Word of God and introduce the power of the Holy Spirit.
Henry and Patricia's goal is to bring restoration to all nations including
the Native Americans. His wife, Patricia is of the Iroquois nation.

Henry & Patricia coordinated large transformation events in New
England under the 'Vision for New England" network which began in
Salem, Ma with the help of Rev Ken Steigler & local pastors. Daystar
programming promoted the events for 2 years. A transformation video
was edited that shares the signs and wonders and miracles that
occurred.

Dr. Henry Lewis is ordained with the Assemblies of God.
Henry is also ordained Rabbi through Asher Intrater from the Revive
Israel Ministries

He is available for speaking.

For More Information

In the US write:

H.A.Lewis
Joshua International

P.O. Box 1799
Maricopa, AZ 85139

Email: Info@halewis.org
Email: Info@ joshua-edu.org

To order or inquire of additional products, visit us online

Website: www.halewis.org
Visit us on face book

Book Cover Artist: Debbie Wheat
Contact: izayu54@yahoo.com

Book Co-coordinators

Grace Miller
Patricia Lewis

Books

A Quest for Spiritual Power - Redeemed from the Curse - testimonial
Choisi Par Le Maitre: En quête de puissance spirituelle - French translation
A Quest for Spiritual Power - Arabic translation
Nimrod - How religions began and how it applies today
Spiritual Opposition to the Five Fold Ministry
The Secret Names of the Strongmen - study material & prayer manual
Jezebel - human or the spirit of baal?
The Dispensation of the Lion and the lamb
The Return of the Days of Noah

Available on Amazon

www.ingramcontent.com/pod-product-compliance
Lightning Source LLC
Chambersburg PA
CBHW071452070426
42452CB00039B/1143